First World War
and Army of Occupation
War Diary
France, Belgium and Germany

38 DIVISION
Divisional Troops
124 Field Company Royal Engineers
3 December 1915 - 7 June 1919

WO95/2547/2

The Naval & Military Press Ltd
www.nmarchive.com
Published in association with The National Archives

Published by

The Naval & Military Press Ltd

Unit 10 Ridgewood Industrial Park,

Uckfield, East Sussex,

TN22 5QE England

Tel: +44 (0) 1825 749494

www.naval-military-press.com

www.nmarchive.com

This diary has been reprinted in facsimile from the original. Any imperfections are inevitably reproduced and the quality may fall short of modern type and cartographic standards.

© Crown Copyright
Images reproduced by permission of The National Archives, London, England, 2015.

Contents

Document type	Place/Title	Date From	Date To
Heading	WO95/2547/3 151 Field Company Royal Engineers		
Heading	124th F.C.R.E. Vol: 3		
Heading	38th Division Divl Engineers 124th Field Coy R.E. Dec 1915-Jun 1919		
Heading	38th Div. 124th F.C.R.E. Vol I 121/7910		
War Diary	Winchester	03/12/1915	03/12/1915
War Diary	Southampton	03/12/1915	03/12/1915
War Diary	Havre	04/12/1915	04/12/1915
War Diary	Aire	05/12/1915	05/12/1915
War Diary	Mametz	06/12/1915	11/12/1915
War Diary	St Venant	12/12/1915	12/12/1915
War Diary	Lacouture	12/12/1915	17/12/1915
War Diary	France B. Serves Sea R.34.d.3 1/2. 2.	18/12/1915	22/12/1915
War Diary	R.34.d.3.2	22/12/1915	31/12/1915
Miscellaneous	Scheme To Improve Line		
War Diary	R.34.d.3.2	01/01/1916	05/01/1916
War Diary	Q.3.a.	06/01/1916	24/01/1916
War Diary	X.5.b.5.4	25/01/1916	29/02/1916
Miscellaneous	To C.R.E. 38th Division		
Miscellaneous	Report on Destruction of Barbed Wire Entanglements by Torpedoes and Gun button.		
Diagram etc	C.H. Brazel, Lieut R.E. for Major R.E. o/c 124th Field Co. R.E.		
Miscellaneous	Report On Experiments Carried Out With No. 13 Service Detonators Using As Earth Return		
Diagram etc	Plan To Show Effects Of Explosions.		
Diagram etc	Plan To Show Entanglements E Position Of The Torpedoes.		
Heading	124 F.C.R.E. Vol 4		
War Diary	X5.b.5.4	01/03/1916	01/03/1916
War Diary	X.20.d	02/03/1916	05/03/1916
War Diary	F.3.d.4.4	06/03/1916	17/04/1916
War Diary	Estairs	18/04/1916	18/04/1916
War Diary	M9.b.5.9	19/04/1916	10/06/1916
War Diary	P.31.c.4.0	11/06/1916	13/06/1916
War Diary	Auchel	14/06/1916	14/06/1916
War Diary	Villers Brulin	15/06/1916	26/06/1916
War Diary	Ransart	27/06/1916	27/06/1916
War Diary	Epecamps	28/06/1916	30/06/1916
Heading	Original War Diary September 1917 124th Field Coy. Royal Engineers 38th Welsh Division		
War Diary	War Diary Of 124th Field Company R.E. 38th (Welsh) Division July. 1916. Vol 8		
War Diary	Val de Maison	01/07/1916	01/07/1916
War Diary	Toutencourt	02/07/1916	03/07/1916
War Diary	Merrincourt l'abbe	04/07/1916	05/07/1916
War Diary	Minden Post Nr Mametz	06/07/1916	07/07/1916
War Diary	Halt Dump	08/07/1916	09/07/1916
War Diary	Minden Post	10/07/1916	10/07/1916
War Diary	Mametz Wood	10/07/1916	11/07/1916

War Diary	F.17.B. Montauban Map	12/07/1916	13/07/1916
War Diary	Rubempre	14/07/1916	14/07/1916
War Diary	Sailly Au Bois	15/07/1916	28/07/1916
War Diary	St Leger Les Authie	29/07/1916	30/07/1916
War Diary	Authieule	31/07/1916	31/07/1916
Heading	War Diary Of 124th Field Company Royal Engineers 38th (Welsh) Division August 1916		
War Diary	Volkerinckhove	01/08/1916	03/08/1916
War Diary	Wormhout	04/08/1916	04/08/1916
War Diary	Elverdinghe	05/08/1916	21/08/1916
War Diary	(Sheet 28 N.W.19.C.3.3	21/08/1916	21/08/1916
War Diary	C.19C 3.3	22/08/1916	31/08/1916
War Diary	War Diary 124th Field Coy. R.E. September 1916		
War Diary	(Sheet 28 N.W) C.19.C.3.3	01/09/1916	01/10/1916
Heading	Original War Diary-October-1916 124 Field Coy. R.E. 38th (Welsh) Dvn.		
War Diary	Map Sheet 28.N.W.C.19.C.3.3	01/10/1916	31/10/1916
Heading	Original War Diary-November 1916. 124th. Field Company, Royal Engineers. 38th. (Welsh) Divn. 30th. November 1916		
War Diary	Sheet. N.W.28.C.19.C.3.3	01/11/1916	30/11/1916
War Diary	December 1916 Original War Diary. 124th Field Company R.E. 38th (Welsh) Division.		
War Diary	Sheet N.W.28 C.19.C.3.3	01/12/1916	12/12/1916
War Diary	C.19.C.3.3	13/12/1916	13/12/1916
War Diary	Merkeghem	14/12/1916	23/12/1916
War Diary	Watten	24/12/1916	30/12/1916
War Diary	Elverdinghe	31/12/1916	31/12/1916
Heading	January 1917 Original War Diary 124th Field Company R.E. 38th (Welsh) Division. 31-1-17 Vol.14		
War Diary	Elverdinghe	01/01/1917	13/01/1917
War Diary	Sheet No. 28 C19.C.2.3	14/01/1917	31/01/1917
Heading	Original War Diary February 1917 124th Field Company R.E. 38th (Welsh) Division Vol.15		
War Diary	Sheet N.W.28 C.19.C.2.3	01/02/1917	23/02/1917
War Diary	C.19.C.2.3	24/02/1917	28/02/1917
Heading	Original War Diary-March 1917. 124th Field Company Royal Engineers 38th (Welsh) Division 31.3.17 Vol.16		
War Diary	Sheet 28 N.W. C.19.C.2.3	01/03/1917	30/03/1917
Heading	Original War Diary-April 1917 124th Field Coy. Royal Engineers 38th (Welsh) Division 30/4/17 Vol.17		
War Diary	Sheet 28.N.W. C.19.C.2.3	01/04/1917	22/04/1917
War Diary	Sheet 28.N.W. C.19.C.3.2	23/04/1917	30/04/1917
Heading	Original War Diary-May 1917 124th Field Company R.E. 38th Welsh Division 31.5.1917		
War Diary	Sheet 28 N.W. C.19.C.3.2	01/05/1917	01/05/1917
War Diary	Sheet 28.N.W. C.19.C.2.3	01/05/1917	31/05/1917
Heading	Original War Diary. June 1917. 124th Field Company Royal Engineers 38th (Welsh) Division 30-6-17 Vol 19		
War Diary	Sheet 28 N.W. C.19.C.2.3	01/06/1917	22/06/1917
War Diary	Watten	23/06/1917	30/06/1917
Heading	July 1917 Original War Diary 124th Field Company. R.E. 38th (Welsh) Division 31.8.17 Vol.20		
War Diary	Sh. Belgium Hazebrouck 5a Boncourt	01/07/1917	24/07/1917
War Diary	Sheet 28 N.W. B.24.b.9.2	25/07/1917	31/07/1917

Heading	Original War Diary-August 1917. 124th Field. Coy. Royal Engineers 38th (Welsh) Division Vol.21		
War Diary	Sheet 28.N.W. C.19.C.2.5	01/08/1917	11/08/1917
War Diary	Sheet 27. E.4.C.8.1	12/08/1917	20/08/1917
War Diary	C.19.C.3.3	21/08/1917	31/08/1917
Map Miscellaneous	Annexe To 124th Field Coy. R.E. War Diary For August 1917	00/08/1917	00/08/1917
War Diary	Sheet 28N.W. B.24.B.9.4	01/09/1917	13/09/1917
War Diary	Sheet 36N.W. Q.19.a.49 1/2	14/09/1917	26/09/1917
War Diary	Sheet 36 N.W. H.15.d.0.1	27/09/1917	15/10/1917
War Diary	Sheet 36N.W.3. H.15.d.0.1	16/10/1917	31/10/1917
War Diary	Sheet 36 N.W.3. H.15.d.1.0	01/11/1917	11/11/1917
War Diary	H.15.d.10	12/11/1917	30/11/1917
Heading	Original War Diary December 1917 124th Field Coy R.E. 38th (Welsh) Division Vol.25		
War Diary	Sheet 36 N.W.3 H.15.d.1.0	01/12/1917	26/12/1917
War Diary	G.17.a.9.z.	27/12/1917	29/12/1917
War Diary	H.19.d.1.1	30/12/1917	31/12/1917
Heading	Original War Diary 124 Field Company R.E. 38th Division Vol 26 January 1918		
War Diary	H.19.d.1.1	01/01/1918	13/01/1918
War Diary	L.29.b.2.6. Sheet 36 N.E	13/01/1918	31/01/1918
War Diary	G.22.b.1.9	01/02/1918	24/02/1918
War Diary	Sheet 36N.W. C.25.C.4.4	25/02/1918	28/02/1918
Heading	Original War Diary March 1918. 124th Field Company Royal Engineers 38th (Welsh) Division		
War Diary	C.25.C.4.4	01/03/1918	31/03/1918
Heading	38th Div. V. Corps. War Diary 124th Field Company, R.E. April 1918		
War Diary	Boesinghem	01/04/1918	02/04/1918
War Diary	Lavicogne	03/04/1918	21/04/1918
War Diary	V.8.b.2.8	22/04/1918	30/04/1918
Heading	Original War Diary May 1918 124th Field Company Royal Engineers 38th (Welsh) Division		
War Diary	V.8.b.2.8	01/05/1918	31/05/1918
Heading	Original War Diary June 1818 124th Field Company Royal Engineers 38th (Welsh) Division Vol 31		
War Diary	V.8.b.2.8. SLL 5/D. S.E.	01/06/1918	11/06/1918
War Diary	P.35.b.7.4	12/06/1918	28/06/1918
War Diary	P.26. Central	29/06/1918	30/06/1918
Heading	Original War Diary July 1918 124th Field Company Royal Engineers 38th Division		
War Diary	P.26. Cen.	01/07/1918	26/07/1918
War Diary	T.6.d.2.2	27/07/1918	31/07/1918
War Diary	Original War Diary 124th Field Company R.E. August Vol.33		
War Diary	T.6.d.22	01/08/1918	09/08/1918
War Diary	Sheet 57 D.S.E. P.36a1.9	10/08/1918	24/08/1918
War Diary	N.15a.7.3	25/08/1918	25/08/1918
War Diary	Shi 57D.S.E. V.15a.7.3	25/08/1918	25/08/1918
War Diary	W11b 80.95	26/08/1918	26/08/1918
War Diary	X10d.5.5	27/08/1918	27/08/1918
War Diary	X13d.2.7	28/08/1918	30/08/1918
War Diary	Shi 57D.S.W X10d.5.5	31/08/1918	11/09/1918
War Diary	P.32.d.2.3	12/09/1918	30/09/1918

War Diary	W.20.a.98	01/10/1918	08/10/1918
War Diary	T.m.b.9.0	09/10/1918	19/10/1918
War Diary	J.35.C.2.8	20/10/1918	30/10/1918
War Diary	J25.C.2.8	31/10/1918	31/10/1918
Heading	Original War Diary November 1918 124th Field Company Royal Engineers 38th (Welsh) Division.		
War Diary	57B.N.E. 21.C.5.4	01/11/1918	03/11/1918
War Diary	Shi 57 A.N.W. A1 b.3.5	04/11/1918	06/11/1918
War Diary	C8.C.9.7	07/11/1918	07/11/1918
War Diary	Shi 51 S.W. M29b.25.85	08/11/1918	09/11/1918
War Diary	Sht. 51 S.E. X.26.b.2.5	10/11/1918	26/11/1918
War Diary	U.21.C.5.4	27/11/1918	30/11/1918
Heading	Original War Diary December 1918 124th Field Company R.E. 38th (Welsh) Division Vol.37		
War Diary	U.21.C5.4	01/12/1918	06/12/1918
War Diary	Querrieu	07/12/1918	31/12/1918
Heading	Original War Diary January 1919 124th Fd. Coy. Royal Engineers 38th (Welsh) Division		
War Diary	Querrieu	01/01/1919	31/01/1919
Heading	Original War Diary February 1919 124th Field Company Royal Engineers 38th (Welsh) Division 38 Div. Vol.39		
War Diary	Querrieu	01/02/1919	16/02/1919
War Diary	Bussy	17/02/1919	28/02/1919
War Diary	Original War Diary 124th Field Coy. R.E. March 1919 38div. Vol. 40		
War Diary	Bussy Les Daours	01/03/1919	31/03/1919
Heading	Original War Diary 124th Field Coy. R.E. April 1919 38 Div. Vol.41		
War Diary	Bussy Les Daours	01/04/1919	08/04/1919
War Diary	Vecquemont.	09/04/1919	07/06/1919

WO95/2547/3
151 Field Company
Royal Engineers

124th F.C. R.E.
Vol: 3

38TH DIVISION
DIVL ENGINEERS

124TH FIELD COY R.E.
DEC 1915 - JUN 1919.

38TH DIVISION
DIVL ENGINEERS

124th F.C.R.E.

Vol: I

124/7910

38 M/5

Dec '15
June '19

Army Form C. 2118.

WAR DIARY
or
INTELLIGENCE SUMMARY.
(Erase heading not required).

124. Field Coy. R.E.

Instructions regarding War Diaries and Intelligence Summaries are contained in F.S. Regs., Part II. and the Staff Manual respectively. Title pages will be prepared in manuscript.

Place	Date	Hour	Summary of Events and Information	Remarks and references to Appendices
Winchester	3/12/15	5-30 a.m.	Marched to Southampton Docks 12 noon. Wet - raining all the way. - Embarked for Havre on	HJK
Southampton	"	about 6.15 p.m.	S.S. "Anglo-Canadian" except 4 Officers & 145 men who embarked on S.S. "Rapide".	
Havre	4/12/15	6-30 a.m.	Unloaded ship - Joined by party from "Rapide" - marched at 12.15 from Docks to No 5 Rest Camp.	HJK
"	"	11.0 p.m.	Marched to Point 3. & entrained for St. Omer.	HJK
Aire	5/12/15	11-55	Continued train journey from St. Omer to Aire. Left Point 3 3-19 a.m. 5/12/15. Arrived Aire 11-55 p.m. 5/12/15. No casualties.	HJK
Allouagne	6/12/15	5 a.m.	Arrived Allouagne after marching from Aire. Had 3 Officers & 105 men. 10 N.C.O.'s N.B. Detached from No 5 Rest Camp Havre to Aire	HJK
Allouagne	7/12/15		Settling in Billets & Parking Tool Carts.	HJK
"	8/12/15		Short Route March. Made arrangements with B⁰⁷ʰ Lm. Mardern 114 "Bgᵈ⁷" for instructing Bgᵈ⁷ in Breastworks & entanglements. Letters read by CRE to Corps. - Appreciation of work done by them in arrangements for Burial of Bodies by H.M. Queen Mary at Winchester & from Lieut. Phillips & Lt. Ln Corroyes.	HJK
Allouagne	9/12/15	9 a.m.	Improving billets, drawing equipment, & packing tool carts & wagons.	
"	"	2 p.m.	Route march via Cergues & Thorenne.	HJK
do.	10/12/15	7 a.m.	1 & 3 Sections instructing 13ᵗʰ & 14ᵗʰ Welsh Regt. in Breastworks, obstacles & General Trench work. No 4 & Hdqrs. doing Rapid firing at short range (50 yards)	HJK

WAR DIARY or INTELLIGENCE SUMMARY.

(Erase heading not required.)

Army Form C. 2118.

Instructions regarding War Diaries and Intelligence Summaries are contained in F.S. Regs., Part II. and the Staff Manual respectively. Title pages will be prepared in manuscript.

Place	Date	Hour	Summary of Events and Information	Remarks and references to Appendices
Allouagne	11/12/15	9 a.m.	Inspection of Kit & equipment.	
		1.30 p.m.	5 Officers & 198 Rank & File marched to St Venant arriving 6 p.m. billeted there for night. 50 Horses & vehicles.	
St Venant	12/12/15	6.0 am	Coy marched via Robecq, Huizes & Lian to Le Touret X roads at R. near Zieverinchove	
Zieverinchove	1.0 p.m.		Coy billeted at R.34. d.32.d. Farm House. Reported to 62 & 46 Bde for instruction	
do	13/12/15	9 a.m.	Cleaning & repairing billet - Inspection of arms & accoutrements	
do			Reported trenches at Factory Post. See work to be carried out by Coy.	
			Section Officers visited same at dusk.	
do	14/12/15	9 a.m.	Coy improving billet, serviceing & cleaning lorries & wagons & drawing stores. Officers visited trenches	
do		3.30 p.m.	Coy proceeded to work at trenches. Employed constructing Sand bag parados Breastwork E. & W. of Factory Rd. Rue du Bois. Finished 9.30 p.m. 016 Cromellino	
do	15/12/15	9 a.m.	Improving billet. Preparing trench stores - Pickets, wire, enuck boards	
do		4 p.m.	Work on Breastwork & Factory Rd. Turning back of latter above water. No Cromellino.	
do	16/12/15		As for 15/12/15 with 100 Wirecutters & swivel Wot. for working party	
do	17/12/15		As for 15/12/15 with 100 Engineers & Wot. do	
do			Searchlight played on party for 5 minutes by enemy	

JAW [signature] Major R.E.

WAR DIARY
or
INTELLIGENCE SUMMARY.

(Erase heading not required.)

Army Form C. 2118.

Place	Date	Hour	Summary of Events and Information	Remarks and references to Appendices
France B. Agnez R.31.d.3½.2.	18/10/15	10 a.m.	Preparing trench duck boards. Paid men. Nos 1 & 4 Sections employed on Brushwork & top of Factory Keep. Nos 2 & 3. on Factory Keep. 6.10 h.m. Lieut Cooper-Sawyer attached to Royal Engineers from this date. No casualties.	JPMK
do	19/10/15	10 a.m.	Preparing trench stores. Church of England Service 11-0 a.m. No trench work. Infantry being relieved. Ye proceeded to Coy HdQrs at Olauety.	JPMK
do	20/10/15	10 a.m.	Preparing trench stores. Ye returned from Olauety 11.30 a.m., having moved at Coy HdQrs on furniture. 38th Division relieving 46th Divn there 4hr. No 1 Section on furniture. Brushworks & dugouts to Ry Cadbury. (see attached sheet No 1). No 2 Section Ditto. S.E. Redt. No 3 Section Factory Keep. No 4 Section Brushwork 2nd Line. Ry Factory Keep Brushwork probably to my left - 1 Infantryman "Generator" killed WK P5. No 3 Section (Sapper) Country very flat. All trenches full of water. Bus Rd by 51st Bde 19th Divn XI Corps 1st Army. Ye inspected all front line trenches - only manned of firestep to along top of Parapet -	Appendix Sheet No 1. JPMK
do	21/10/15	10 a.m.	Preparing trench stores. Working parties cancelled owing to wet weather -	
do	22/10/15	10 a.m.	Preparing trench stores. Arranged with Ye 94, 670 G R for Officers to visit S.P. Lieut Guynne on S.P. at Neuve Chapelle.	JPMK

Army Form C. 2118.

WAR DIARY
or
INTELLIGENCE SUMMARY.
(Erase heading not required.)

Instructions regarding War Diaries and Intelligence Summaries are contained in F. S. Regs., Part II. and the Staff Manual respectively. Title pages will be prepared in manuscript.

Place	Date	Hour	Summary of Events and Information	Remarks and references to Appendices
R.34.d.3.2	22/12/15	9 a.m.	Preparation of Trench Stores. "Dug-outs" No 1 - 2 Sections on Front line Breastworks & "Dug-outs"	
		4 p.m.	" " Fatigue Rept & Breastworks. Working parties 200 - 7th E. Lancs -	
			No 3 & 4 " " Work parties at grm. enemy & two bombing attacks on our right. Enemy Machine Guns & Snipers busy. No casualties	
do.	23/12/15	10 a.m.	Preparation of Trench Stores. Continued work of 22/12/15. No casualties	
do.	24/12/15	10 a.m.	do for 23/12/15.	
do.	25/12/15	10 a.m.	Preparation of Stores & harness. - Christmas day - No working parties.	
do.	26/12/15	10 a.m.	Preparation of Trench Stores. Afternoon & evening as for 22/12/15.	
do.	27/12/15	10 a.m.	do. Afternoon Nos 1 & 2 Sections continued improvement of Front line Trenches. No 3 Section on Factory Keep. No 4 constructing O.P. at Chocolat Menier Corner. Part of No 4 action 25 N.C.O.s on O.P. at CHATEAU REDOUBT KETTLE NEUVE CHAPPELE Rue du Bois.	
do.	28/12/15	10 a.m.	do for yesterday. No 1 Section 1 casualty Pte Roderick R 6755 wounded by Shrapnel on Cadbury Comn Trench on return from work.	
	29/12/15	10 a.m.	as for yesterday. No 1 Section 1 Casualty. Pte H. Cox 6808 wounded left arm. M.G. bullet. returning from front line.	✓ R.M.R.

2353 Wt. W2514/1454 700,000 5/15 D. D. & L.   A.D.S.S./Forms/C. 2118.

WAR DIARY
or
INTELLIGENCE SUMMARY.

Army Form C. 2118.

Place	Date	Hour	Summary of Events and Information	Remarks and references to Appendices
R.34 d.22.	30/1/15	10.0 am	Rylanctures of trench Stores. No 1 & 2 Sections continued work on Front line parapets & Dugouts - Part of No 3 Section continued pracing & revetment of parapets in Factory Rd. 1 Officer & 50 men employed on O.P. at Neuve Chappelle & Chocolate Menier Corner Rue du Bois.	
do	31/12/15	10 am	Preparation of trench Stores - Bombing Practice - Infantry Working Parties Cancelled & owing to Brigade changing.	

J.R. Winterwood Major RE
OC 124 Fd Co RE

SCHEME TO IMPROVE LINE

Sketch No 1

The front line is now wet in many places owing to the general rise of water, and it is intended to improve conditions by taking in hand the construction of islands, in which the ground level at the foot of the parapet will be raised clear of the water, good bomb-proof shelter provided for the garrison, the parapet heightened & made bullet-proof, and a parados built.

It is impossible to treat every island in exactly the same way, but the following will explain the principle, and enable everyone to cooperate in the work.

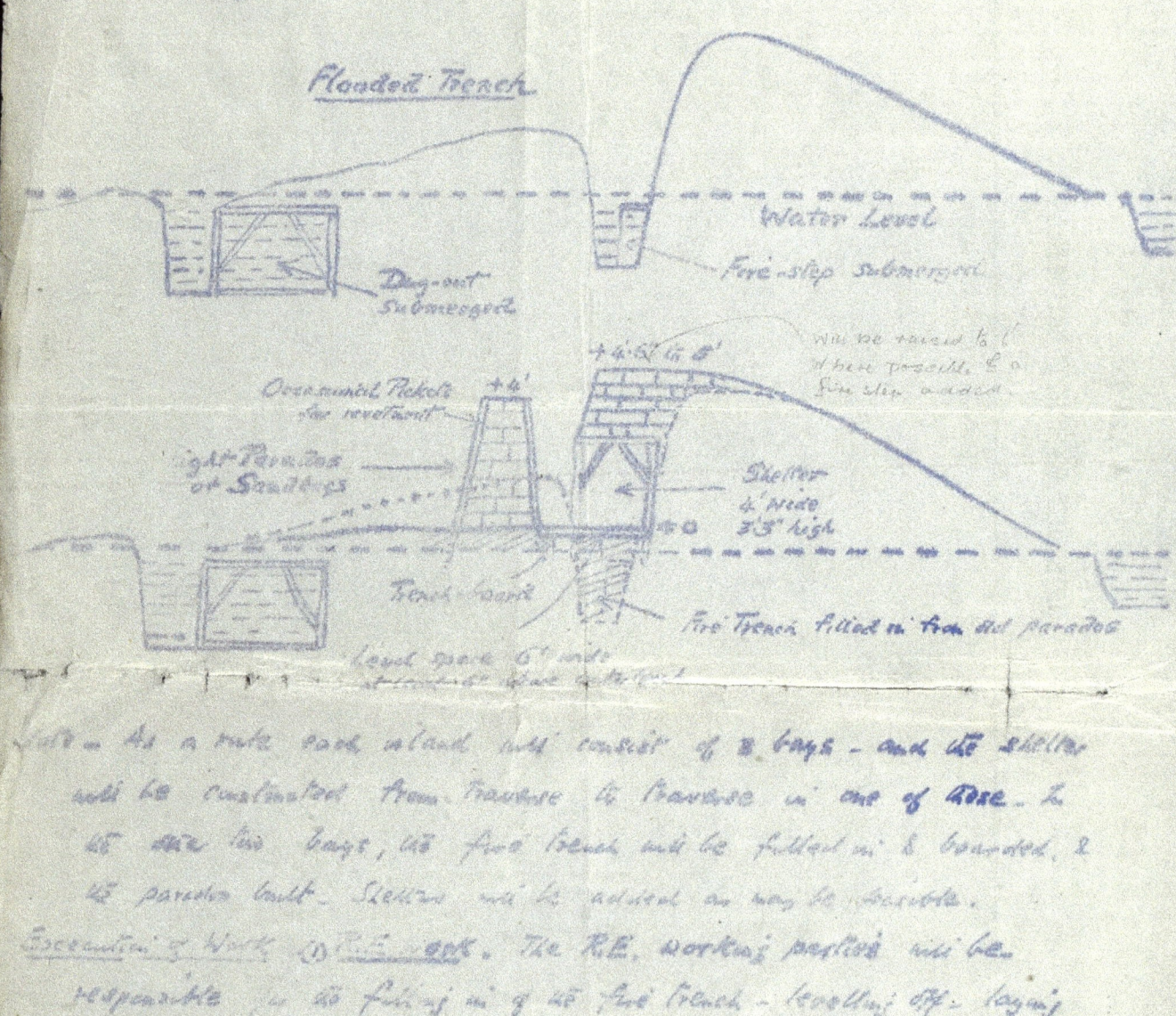

Flooded Trench

Note — As a rule each island will consist of 3 bays — and the shelter will be constructed from traverse to traverse in one of these. In the other two bays, the fire trench will be filled in & boarded, & the parados built. Shelters will be added as may be possible.

Execution of Work (1) R.E. work. The R.E. working parties will be responsible for the filling in of the fire trench — levelling off — laying trench boards, & building the shelter, & placing 1st row of sandbags on same.

(2) Infantry. The Infantry holding the line will be responsible for building up the sandbags on top of the shelter to full height, and for building the light parados — including the carrying up of sandbags for the same.

R.F.A. Butterworth
Major R.E.
O.C. 82nd Field Co. R.E.

16th Dec. 1915.

WAR DIARY or INTELLIGENCE SUMMARY

Army Form C. 2118.

124th Fd. C.R.E. — *(written sideways)*

Place	Date	Hour	Summary of Events and Information	Remarks
R.3.4.d.3.R	1.1.16	10.0am	Preparation of trench stores. No working parties available for N°s 1,2 & 3 Sections owing to Bn. reaching. N° 4 Section work on N° 4 O.P. Rue du Bois.	
R.3.4.d.3.2	2.1.16	10.0am	Preparation of Trench Stores. N° 1 Section Continued improvement of front line at S.15.d.7.4. Sappers 12 Infantry 58. N° 2 Section improvement of front line & construction of M.G. emplacements in front line. Sappers 15 Infantry 60. N° 3 Section Repairing Factory Keep. Sq. d.7.7. & constructing M.G. emplacements. Sappers 14 Infantry 100. N° 4 Section construction of the N° 4 O.P. Rue du Bois. S.15.a.6.3. Sappers 25 working in two shifts.	
R.3.4.d.3.2	3.1.16	10.0am	G.E.M on Sqt M. Hitzer 82300. Charged with "while on Active Service being drunk on duty" on Dec 19th 1915. N° 1 Section Improvement of front line at S.15.d.7.4. N° 2 Section Continued improvement of front line & dugouts. N° 3 Section Continued work in Factory Keep. N° 4 Section The N° 4 O.P. & M.G. emplacement completed. Rue du Bois completed.	
R.3.4.d.3.2	4.1.16	10.0am	Preparation of Trench Stores. N°s 1.2.3 Section in fit 3-1-16. N° 4 Section Reconstruction of O.P. Rivetts Ravage. Rue du Bois. Received orders from C.R.E. 38th Div to proceed to 2.3.a on 5.1.16. Wired details at 2.3.a. 15 Artizans & fat wagons.	
R.3.4.d.3.2	6.1.16	10.0am	Packed wheels & in readiness for move. N° 2 Section H5 men 12 horses sent as advance party to 2.3.a. Received orders from C.R.E. 38th Div for party of 2 Officers & 50 men to remain to proceed with O.P. work, to be attached to 87th & 88th Bgde R.F.A. NB working parties available owing to Battalion changes.	Delivered Lloyd RE

2353 Wt. W.2544/1454 700,000 5/15 D.D.&L. A.D.S.S./Forms/C.2118.

WAR DIARY 124th Fd Co. R.E.

Army Form C. 2118.

Place	Date	Hour	Summary of Events and Information	Remarks and references to Appendices
Q.5.a	6.1.16	10.0am	Reported R 3.H d 3 2 at 10.0 am. Arrived Q.5.a 12-30 pm. Officers 3. Men 100. Horses Mules H.6. Commenced improvement of billets.	
Q.5.a	7.1.16	10.0am	Improvement of Billets. Bombing practice. Received Result of G.C.M. held on Sep 1st May on 28.3 on 2-1-16. Prisoner found Guilty. Sentence Reduced to Ranks. Route March. 2-0 pm Parade. Company Pay Certain Hand.	
Q.3.a	8.1.16	10.0am	Improvement of Billets. Repairs to Vehicles. Concert arranged for men at 6-30 pm to 8.0 pm.	
Q.3.a	9.1.16	10.0am	Improvement of Billets. Divine Service. Repairs to Vehicles. Bombing Practice. Walk in Brigade Boots on G.S.C.	
Q.3.a	10.1.16	10.0am	Improvement of Billets &c. Repairing Vehicles.	
Q.3.a	11.1.16	10.0am	Improvement of Billets. Checking Stores.	
Q.3.a	12.1.16	10.0am	Checking Stores. Constructing Experimental cooking ovens. (See attached diagrams).	
Q.3.a	13.1.16	10.0am	Checking Stores. Constructing Ovens. Received instructions to carry out experiments on Wire Entanglements with Defences made with Ammonal and Gun Cotton.	
Q.3.a	14.1.16	10.0am	Continued Construction of Ovens & entanglements for the above mentioned experiments and making of plankets from Forest of Nieppe, & bricks from Tonquette.	
Q.3.a	15.1.16	10.0am	As above for 14-1-16. Constructing Brick horse standing.	
Q.3.a	16.1.16	10.0am	As for 15-1-16.	
Q.3.a	17.1.16	10.0am	As for 15-1-16. Applied for 2 tons fuel to test ovens constructed as above.	

H.W.Williams Major R.E.

WAR DIARY or INTELLIGENCE SUMMARY

Army Form C. 2118.

124 "TWELVE"

A.B. M?Pherson Lloyd M?

Place	Date	Hour	Summary of Events and Information	Remarks and references to Appendices
Q3.a	18-1-16	10.0am	Continued construction of Brick Lime Storage. Wire entanglements & Ovens. Received authority to draw 2 tons of fuel to test ovens.	
Q3.a	19-1-16	10.00	Entered with Scrat Stanage. Wire Entanglements. Made preliminary test with ovens.	
Q3.a	20-1-16	10.00am	As above. Received orders to move to X5 b. Central Sheet 36A SE on 22 at 2pm. Route via Cabones, Paradis, Zeloobes. R28 d. 6.6.16 x 5 b central.	
Q3.a	21-1-16	10.00am	Completed Wire Entanglements. Carried out first experiment on enlarging end with Ammonal Torpedo (tube?). Colonel Price + Major Rice 170 11? G.S. ——— 38th Div were present.	
Q3.a	22-1-16	10.00am	Experiments on Wire Entanglements with Ammonal & Guncotton Torpedoes. Packed vehicles in readiness for move. Received orders to move on 24th instead of 22nd.	
Q3.a	23-1-16	10.0am	Cleaning Billets. Billetting.	
Q3.a	24-1-16	10.0 a	As for B5th 19b. Left Q3.a at 8-15 am 24-1-16.	
X5 b5.4	25-1-16	10.0am	Arrived X5 B5.4 at 11-30 am. 24-1-16. Arranged Billets. Visited various portions of line which we were taking over.	
X5 b5.4	26-1-16	10.00am	Arranging R.E. Stores. Inspection of front line from Somme Comm. Sap Trenches & Lunques Rue Nationale. Worked Steam & Cathury Communication Trench.	
X5 b5.4	27-1-16	10.0am	Inspection of Billets. Worked at Farm Comm. & Triangular Rue one August Road in Rifle Butt Shrapnel Inspected further work on Cathury Communication Trench. Drainage at Rue des Bois continued.	

2353 Wt. W2544/1454 700,000 5/15 D.D.&L. A.D.S.S./Forms/C. 2118.

WAR DIARY
INTELLIGENCE SUMMARY

Army Form C. 2118.

124th Fd Coy RE

Place	Date	Hour	Summary of Events and Information	Remarks and references to Appendices
X5 b 5.4	28.1.16	10.0 a.m.	Work in Company HQ yard. No infantry working parties available owing to Batt Relief. Work at Gun Coen or Zuaque Rue, & on Cadbury Communication Trench. Infiltration of water from Rue de Bois to Zollern Rue Keep. Billet shelled between 1 & 2 p.m.	Witnessed by me A.R.K.
X5 b.5.4, 29.1.16	29.1.16	10.0 a.m.	Improvement of drainage at gun emplacements & Zuaque Rue and improvement of Cadbury track with wire netting. Continued pile stops in Bkt Keep & Hors. Dug out in Tube Station. Dug out in Rear Com Tel. Infiltration of Tramway between Gun b Shaw & Tube Station. Continued drainage of Rue de Bois. Billet shelled 3.0 p.m.	
X5 b.8.4	30.1.16	10.00 a.m.	Work on Gun Comn. continued & Zuaque Rue northwards. Revised parapet in Rope Keep.	
X5 b5.4	31.1.16	10.0 a.m.	Visited by M+G & G of North Army before Committee. Work on Gun Comn & 11 f Zuaque Rue. Parapets raised rear air freet & his machine g un emplacements commenced. Continued work on drainage from Rue de Bois to Hollow Embankment.	
X5 B5.4	1-2.16	10 a.m.	Work on Trench line west of Gun Com north of Zuaque Rue. Machine gun emplacement in Rope Keep. No infantry working parties available owing to Battalion relief. Arrival of draft.	

No. 1020 bg. S & of p. Balto.

Army Form C. 2118.

WAR DIARY
or
INTELLIGENCE SUMMARY.
(Erase heading not required.)

124th Fd. Co. R.E.

Instructions regarding War Diaries and Intelligence Summaries are contained in F. S. Regs., Part II. and the Staff Manual respectively. Title pages will be prepared in manuscript.

Place	Date	Hour	Summary of Events and Information	Remarks and references to Appendices
X.5.b.5.A.	2.2.16	10.0am	Work on front line S of Ian Cavan. 1 N of Quinque Rue. Battenge in old Brit line. Work on Rifle Keep, Tube Station. Breastwork Repairs to Whole Front U.P. work on drains. Boats supplied from entry departments non Villas.	
X.5.b.5.A.3.2.16.		10.0am	Front line improvement as above. Turning covers from 3'-0" to 7'-0" in Princess Road. One H.E. 4.9" dropped near killed 3.0 pm.	
X.5.b.5.A.4.2.16.		10.0am	Front line improvement as above. Work in Sapp Post. Dressing Post. Tube Station. Rifle keep. Salvage & work in Old Brit line. Repairs to Pumps at S.P. at 91. Renewing of screen on Princess Road.	
X.5.6.b.4.5.2.16.		10.0 am	Battalion change. No working parties available. Company employed during day making stores for trench use - dugout frames, signboards, latrine seats. Emplacements for M.G. arranged between posts Nos 10, 11, 7 & 8, & 1 & 2, in conjunction with M.G. officer. Road repairs at X.5.b.5.4. Boiler baths erected at S.P. d. T.S.	
X.5.6.b.5.A.6.11.16.		10.0 am	Front line improvement. Left Section Right Sector S. of Farm Corner. Connecting up Pots Nos 7 & 8 & Nos 12 & 13. Revetting erection of hurdle traverses between Nos 14 & 15. N of Farm Corner. Front Line. Right Sector. Right Sector Connecting between posts 12 & 13. Fri. Steps commenced & cook house built to O.C. Improvements to following keeps continues Sapp. Post. Dead Cow, Rifle and Tube Station. Salvage in old British line.	

F.M. Wodehouse Major R.E.

WAR DIARY

Army Form C. 2118.

INTELLIGENCE SUMMARY. 124th Fd. Co. R.E.

Place	Date	Hour	Summary of Events and Information	Remarks and references to Appendices
X.5.b.5.4.	6.11.16	10.00 a.m.	(Cont.) Improvements to Bournville Breastwork. Drainage continued and erection of hurdle fence along Princes Road carried on. Lieut C.H. Brazil appointed 2nd in Pl. adjt. left the Company	
X.5.b.5.4.	7.11.16	10.0 a.m.	Front line improvement as last. Posts Nos. 7+8, 12+13, 14+15 (Left Section) Nos 6+7, 12+13 (Right Section) being gradually linked up. The 20 yds interval number plates 1 to 20 used. Rapid hurdle screen to Princes Rd continued. Improvement to Bournville Breastwork. Works to abovementioned posts continued. 40 N.C.O.s + men of 13th, 14th, 15th + 16th Batt. R.W.F. attached to this Coy for front line drainage under 2/Lt Llewellyn - 19 2/Lt Welch. arrived + billeted at X.5.b.5.4.	
X.5.b.5.4. & 11.16	8.11.16	10.0 a.m.	Front line improvement - Left Section - New post built + garrisons between Nos 12+13. Revetting fire bays between Nos 7+8. Right Section. Linking up Nos 12+13. Screen down Princes Rd continued. Drainage work to posts carried on. Drainage from Rue de Bois to Halfway completed. Opened new drain across the Rue du Bois at Rum Corner and drain along Rue du Bois from Rum to Chocolate Menin Corner deepened. A fall of 14 inches was observed. When completed this will self to empty area drained by Ancy Canal	
X.5.b.5.4	9.11.16	10 a.m.	Brigade Relief. No working parties available. Bournville Breastwork and the posts	

R. Kirkwood Ellyn?

WAR DIARY
or
INTELLIGENCE SUMMARY

Army Form C. 2118.

P4 1/5 Fd. C.R.E.

Place	Date	Hour	Summary of Events and Information	Remarks and references to Appendices
X.5.b.5.4.	9.11.16	10-0 a.m.	(Cont) above mentioned. Company employed. Preparing M.G. emplacements. Dug out frames etc and Revetting material.	
X.5.b.5.4.	10.11.16	10 a.m.	Works during day in yard preparing stores for trench use. Work on tramway during the day. Raising sliding rails. Works to posts - dugs. Albert. Dead Cow and Rope Keep. Improvement to revetting and dug out accommodation. Cleaning out Pipe Trench. Screens to Princes Rd. Improvement to Bouzincourt breastwork and drainage. Usual improvement work to Front Line.	
X.5.b.5.4.	11.11.16	10 a.m.	As for yesterday. Brigadier 114th Brigade & C.R.E. visited lines.	
X.5.b.5.4.	12.11.16	10 a.m.	As for 10.11.16.	
X.5.b.5.4.	13.11.16	10 a.m.	Front line improvements. New M.G. emplacement at Post No 2 Left Section Right Section. New dug out between No's 12 & 13 Right Section Right Section. Fire steps & bomb stores. Works to Post steps. Dogs. Rope. and Pipe Trench. Screen raised along Princes Road.	
X.5.b.5.4.	14.11.16	10 a.m.	Front Line improvement. Revetting and thickening Fire bays & Traverses. Left Section Right Section. Snipers emplacement built in Traverse. Right Section. Right section. M.G. Emplacement built. Work to Rope Keep Sandbagging parapet and building dug	

R.R. Kirkwood Major R.E.

Army Form C. 2118.

WAR DIARY
or
INTELLIGENCE SUMMARY.
(Erase heading not required.)

Army Form C. 2118.

124 & Fd. Co. R.E.

Instructions regarding War Diaries and Intelligence Summaries are contained in F. S. Regs. Part II. and the Staff Manual respectively. Title pages will be prepared in manuscript.

Place	Date	Hour	Summary of Events and Information	Remarks and references to Appendices
			out. Pipe Communication Trench. work continues. Hostile artillery shells dropped at different spots round the billet, during the afternoon of 15%. Difficult to say what target this was intended for.	
X.5.b.6.4	15.11.16	10 a.m.	Front line improvement. Right Section, R. Sector. Parapets raised & thickened. Left Section R. Sector- do. to Right. M.G. Emplacement at P.P. 2 Completed. C.H.Q.s Completed at P.P.8. Pipe Trench & Rope Keeps work continued.	
X.5.b.5.4	16.11.16	10 a.m.	Front line improvement. R. Sector. R. Section. Parapets raised & thickened. L. Section. Right Section do to Right. M.G. Emplacement at S.21.C.8.8. Screens & Princes Rd. Pipe Trench & Rope Keeps work continued.	
X.5.b.5.4	17.11.16	10 a.m.	do. to 16th. Line from Plumb St to Farm Corner- taken over from 123 Field Co. R.E. including St Vaast dumps. Front line from S.10.d.1.8 to S.15.d.9½.0. Following - Communication Trenches: Haryana, Cohae St, Vine St, Bond St, Cockshurst, and Pall Mall. Following Keeps- News, Edward, St Vaast, Augell, Factory, Cohae, Richebourg, Rugo, Boris & Grotto. No working parties available.	
X.5.b.5.4	18.11.16	10 a.m.	do. to 16th. Work commenced at Cohae St. Cockshurst. Rangers & Bond St. Revetting and restoring Communication trenches.	

H.M. Lockwood Major R.E.

Army Form C. 2118.

WAR DIARY
or
INTELLIGENCE SUMMARY.
(Erase heading not required.)

1/4 &Fd Co RE

Instructions regarding War Diaries and Intelligence Summaries are contained in F.S. Regs., Part II. and the Staff Manual respectively. Title pages will be prepared in manuscript.

Place	Date	Hour	Summary of Events and Information	Remarks and references to Appendices
X.5.6.5.4.	19.11.16	10 a.m.	Unit Started in addition.	
X.5.6.5.4.	20.11.16	10 a.m.	As for 18th. Enemy aircraft busy during evening noticeably at 10.30 p.m. Two bombs dropped near billet at 11.15 p.m.	
X.5.6.5.4.	21.2.16	10 a.m.	As for 18th. Firstly connected 6 listening post at extreme end of Sap at Duav Head. Two Sections of 209th Field Coy RE attached for instruction.	
X.5.6.	22.2.16	10 a.m.	As for 18th. Constructing wire entanglement in front.	
X.5.6.	23.2.16	10 a.m.	As for 18th. New dug out for OC Coy at head of Sap Ct Completed.	
X.5.6.5.4.	24.2.16	10 a.m.	As for 18th. Heavy fall of snow interfered with RE work. Two Companies of 19th Battn Northumberland Fusiliers attached & employed on Rope Trench & Bonneville Breastwork under this Coy's Supervision. Erecting OPS at Factory Leicester Lounge, & MG emplacement No.3, also 18 pdr gun emplacement at S.14.C.15.	
X.5.6.5.4.	25.2.16	10 a.m.	As for 24th.	
X.5.6.5.4.	26.2.16	10 a.m.	Repairing trench stores & work in billet, R.E. work in front line as prevented owing to snow & severe frost.	
X.5.6.5.4.	27.2.16	10 a.m.	Work on Leicester Lounge, Factory & Savoy OPS & M.G. emplacement No 3 advanced. Loopes of Trenches between Posts 9 & 10 Left Section, Right Sector raised to 4'.0", 9 Turnples erected	

R.N. Wodward Major RE

Army Form C. 2118.

124th Fd. Co R.E

WAR DIARY
or
INTELLIGENCE SUMMARY.
(Erase heading not required.)

Place	Date	Hour	Summary of Events and Information	Remarks and references to Appendices
X5 b5 d 29.2.16	29.2.16	10 a.m.	Between Farm Corner & listening post, & earth bags up in front of shelters. Work on Pipe Trench continued. Clearing & improving Byex St. Bond St. Nugget St. Vine St. Rangers Trenches, & erecting screen over at Boris road calcining huts. (4 men of Company wounded) (1 man killed & 6 may wounded of working party).	
X5 b5 d 28.2.16	28.2.16	10 a.m.	Same as 27th. Repairs to favery L.P. finished. Duckboard track laid between Lulu Station & Batth. Headquarters at Indian Village. (10.5 S.W. Bordeaux on Right.)	
X5 b5 d 29.2.16	29.2.16	10 a.m.	Same as 27th. Forming M.G. emplacement at Rope Kept. First 1 inch trench board track between Lulu Station & B.H.Q. of 6pt Batth. Central Sector. M.M.G. emplacement at P.D.Honor S1 c 53 completed. Stocktaking at dumps at X5 b5 u & S'Haast, clearing billets, loading Coy. Stores, preparatory to handing over to 2281st Field Coy. on March 1st.	

R.N.Kirkwood Major R.E
[signature] 124 Fd Co R.E

124th Fd Co RE

To C.R.E. 38th Division.

Sir,

Destruction of Barbed Wire Entanglements

I beg to submit herewith reports on experiments carried out in blowing up wire entanglements by means of torpedoes of Ammonal in pipes and Guncotton slabs on timber:-

Explosives used.
1. Ammonal in 2" Galvanised Iron pipes containing 1.3 lbs per foot run.
2. Guncotton in slabs fixed in grooved timber; charge 2 lbs per foot run.

Effect.
Ammonal. Good.
Guncotton. Poor.

Conclusions.
1. The torpedo must run the full depth of the entanglement to be cleared.
2. The height or type of the wire does not affect the result.
3. The best results will always be obtained from explosions contained in pipes, as this gives the effect of a tamped charge as against the untamped guncotton (Apart from the pipe fragments assisting in cutting the wire.)

(4) Any large numbers of torpedoes to be fired simultaneously should be fired electrically, preferably two in parallel to each line from the exploder. Any increase in this number would increase the chances of the whole circuit being broken.

Remarks.

(1) A 18'6" x 2" diam G.I. pipe filled with Ammonal weighs 98 lbs. Any increase over 20ft long would become unwieldy and difficult to handle.

(2) Very accurate reconnaissance of enemy wire to be blown up, would have to be made, to be certain of a passage being cleared all the way through it.

I also attach details of experiments we have made in blowing up charges with a single wire from Exploder and a return through earth. This might be useful should one wire become badly damaged.

I am,
Sir,
Your Obedient Servant
(Sgd) J.P. Kirkwood, Major R.E.
O.C. 124th Field Coy. R.E.

Report on Destruction of Barbed Wire Entanglements by Torpedoes of Ammonal and Gun Cotton.

Description of Torpedoes

Ammonal Torpedo

This consists of a Wrought Iron pipe 2" internal diameter 18'6" long. One end is closed by means of a wooden plug firmly driven in. The pipe is then filled with 25 lbs Ammonal, care being taken that the Ammonal settles firmly leaving no air spaces. The other end is closed as follows (See fig Plate I):—

The ordinary thimble is partly closed at one end. A wooden plug made to a good driving fit and having a hole bored through to take the detonator.

When the pipe is filled, the plug is fitted, and the detonator hole is closed by means of a small wooden plug which can be easily withdrawn. The thimble is then screwed on over the wooden plug and tighted up with a pipe wrench. The torpedo weighs 98 lbs.

To facilitate carrying, a sling of 1" cordage is placed at each end.

To fire the Torpedo.

Electrically.

Withdraw the small wooden plug from the hole in the large plug, and insert a No. 13 Electric detonator which has been connected up to the cable from the exploder. The small plug is then replaced holding the two lead wires of the detonator firmly in the hole. The torpedo is then ready to be fired.

By Fuse & No 8 detonator.

Withdraw the small wooden plug from the hole in the large wooden plug and insert a No 8 Detonator which has been attached to a length of fuse. The small plug is

I

then replaced holding the fuse firmly in the hole. The torpedo is then ready to be fired.

Gun Cotton Torpedo is constructed as follows:—
See fig.

A groove 20 ft long 3" x 3/8" deep is cut in a piece of deal 21 ft x 4" x 2". The ends are shaped off to resemble a skid.

40 Gun Cotton slabs are laid in the groove and a primer is placed in the end slab of gun-cotton. The whole is then firmly secured by wrapping cotton tape around the slabs and the 4" x 2" timber. To facilitate carrying a sling of 1" cordage is arranged at either ends as in sketch. The torpedo weighs 50 lbs.

To fire the Torpedo.
① Electrically.

A No 13 Electric Detonator is connected up to the cables which run back to the Exploder. The Detonator is then placed in the hole in the primer in the first G.C. slab and the torpedo is ready to be fired.

② By fuse and No 8 Detonator

The end of the instantaneous fuse is bored in the red braid and the quick match is placed in the detonator and the end closed up. The detonator is placed in the hole in the primer and the torpedo is ready to fire.

The Barbed Wire. A barbed wire entanglement was prepared of several different combinations of High Wire Entanglement, Low Wire Entanglement & Knife Rests. The depth of the entanglement was in every case 20 ft. The arrangement of the various combinations can best be seen in the sketch. Fig.   Plate 2.

Experiment I (Jan. 20th 1916. 2.30pm)

In this case an Armoural Torpedo was used and the entanglement was composed of half High Wire & half Low wire. The torpedo was fired electrically.

The width of the lane cut was 10 ft. The wire in one pile was not cut, evidently owing to the Torpedo being only 18'6" long and the entanglement 20 feet deep.

The ground where the torpedo had been was disturbed for 2' on either side, and about 1 ft deep. The lane cut was completely cleared of wire and pickets except the side wires mentioned above.

Experiment II (Jan. 21st 1916. 10am).

Two Armoural Torpedoes were placed under the entanglement 20 ft. apart. The entanglement was composed of Low wire, Knife Rest, & High wire. It was intended to fire the two torpedoes simultaneously by electrical methods, & the two No 13 electric detonators were connected in series. However only one detonator fired. The other detonator was afterwards fired independently. The total width of the lane cut by the two torpedoes was 33 ft. Again the side wires were not cut as in experiment I.

Note. The fact that the one No 13 detonator failed to fire can only be attributed to the varying sensitivity of the detonators, one detonator having fired and broken the electric current before the other had time to act.

Experiment III.

Two Gun Cotton torpedoes were used in this experiment. The torpedoes were placed at

30ft apart. The entanglement was composed of High wire and low wire Knife Rests. The torpedoes were fired electrically, two No 13 electric detonators being connected in parallel. Both torpedoes fired simultaneously but a lane of only 12ft wide was cut by one and only a small clearance was made in the centre by the other. The side wires were not cut, although the torpedo was 20ft long. The ground on each side of where the torpedo was, was disturbed for a width of 3ft & 1ft deep.

Experiment No 4.

Two Ammonal torpedoes were used and placed 20ft apart. The entanglement was composed of High wire, Low wire, & Knife rests. The torpedoes were fired by No 8 Service Detonators and Instantaneous fuse. Both torpedoes fired simultaneously. A lane of 7ft wide was cut in the wire. The side wires again were not cut.

Experiment No 5

One Ammonal torpedo was used. The entanglement was composed of all low wire. The torpedo was fired electrically. A lane 20ft wide was cut. The end wires were not cut.

Method of attack with Ammonal or Guncotton Torpedoes

The torpedo is carried up to within 50 yards of the enemy's wire by two men, a third man following with the electric cable & No 13 electric detonator. On reaching the 50 yards limit the men have to crawl along the ground pulling the torpedo after them. The third man also following crawling. On reaching the enemy's wire the torpedo is pushed in under the wire. The third man inserts the detonator which is connected to the cable, & the torpedo is ready to be fired. The exploder could be placed in a listening post infront of our lines or even taken right back to our front line where the enemy's lines are near ours.

(Sgd) J. R. N. Kirkwood Major R.E.
O.C. 134th Field Coy R.E.

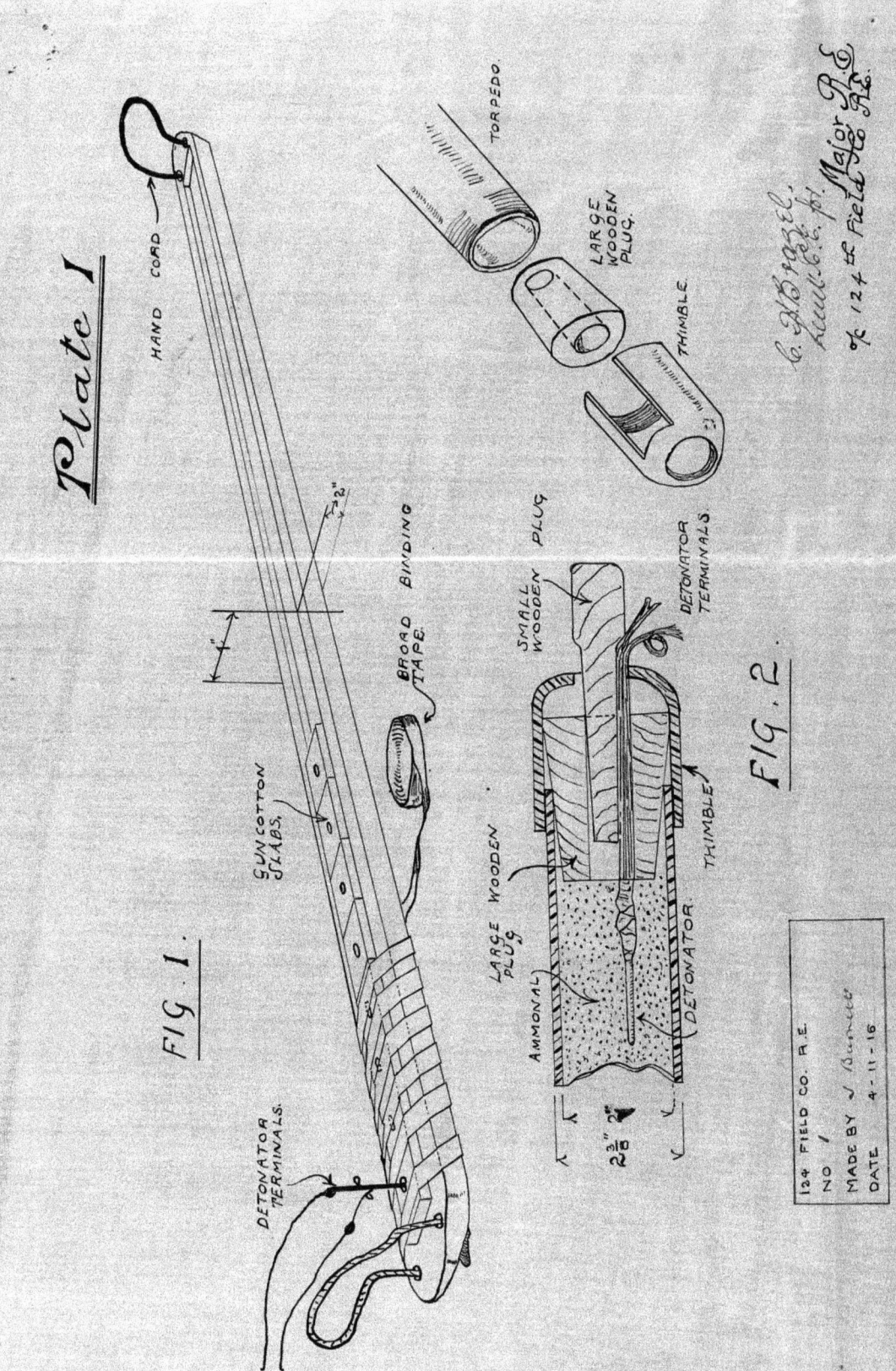

Report on Experiments carried out with No 13 Service Detonators using an Earth Return

In these experiments, instead of using a return wire, one terminal of the detonator was earthed, and one terminal of the exploder was earthed. See diagram.

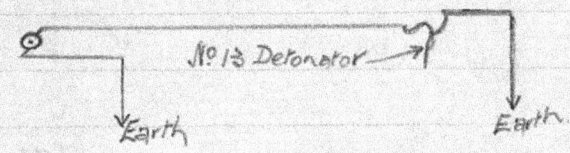

An ordinary Jack knife was used as an Earth Plate.

The following results were obtained:-
1. One No. 13 Detonator fired at 55 yards.
2. Two No 13 Detonators connected in series fired at 100 yards
3. Two No 13 Detonators connected in parallel fired at 100 yards
4. One No. 13 Detonator fired at 200 yards
5. Two No. 13 Detonators in parallel fired at 200 yards (2ⁿᵈ attempt).

In all cases the "Earth" was extremely good owing to the very damp nature of the ground.

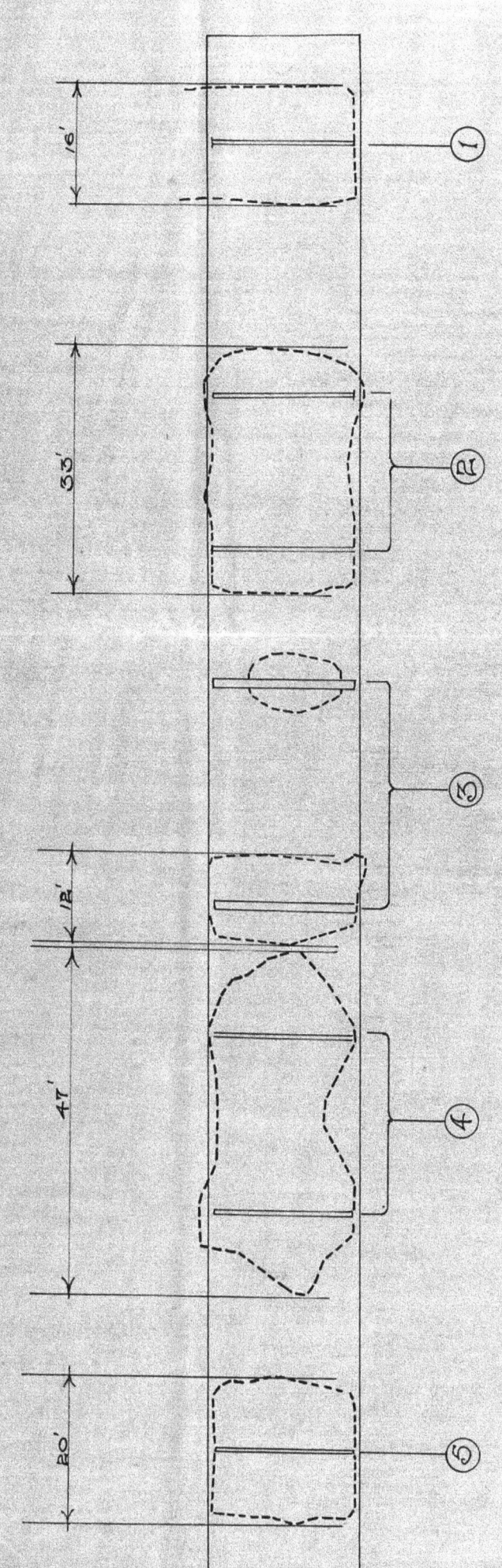

PLAN TO SHOW ENTANGLEMENTS & POSITION OF THE TORPEDOES.

Plate B.

Reference.
- LOW WIRE ....
- HIGH WIRE ....
- KNIFE RESTS ....
- AMMONAL TORPEDO ....
- GUNCOTTON TORPEDO ....

① LOW WIRE 42' / 1'6" HIGH.

④ HIGH WIRE. 30' / AVERAGE — 4'6"

③ KNIFE RESTS. 38' / LOW WIRE.

③ HIGH WIRE 40' / LOW WIRE 1'6"

② APRON FENCE, KNIFE RESTS & LOW WIRE.

① HIGH WIRE 4'6" 30' / & LOW WIRE 1'6"

Scale of feet.

Major R.E.
% 124 Field Co. R.E.

38

124 JCRE

Vol 4

WAR DIARY or INTELLIGENCE SUMMARY

Army Form C. 2118.

(Erase heading not required.)   **124th Field Company, Royal Engineers**

Place	Date	Hour	Summary of Events and Information	Remarks and references to Appendices
X5 & 5.H	1-3.16	10 a.m.	Handing over reports on fractures & progress of works in hand and contemplated, particulars of stores on hand and dealt with at X5 & 54 & stores charge to O.C. 92nd Field Coy. R.E. Company moved to new billets at X 20 d at 7 a.m.	Witnessed Major R.E. 124th Field Coy R.E.
X 20 d.	2.3.16	10 a.m.	Improving billets	
X 20 d.	3.3.16	10 a.m.	do	
X 20 d.	4.3.16	10 a.m.	do	
X 20 d.	5.3.16	10 a.m.	do	
23 d.4.4	6.3.16	10 a.m.	Moved to billet at 23 d.4.4 at 11 a.m. on 5th - Improving billet	
23 d 4.4	7.3.16	10 a.m.	Improving billet, erecting workshops, stables, etc.	
23 d 4.4	8.3.16	10 a.m.	Same as for 7th	
23 d 4.4	9.3.16	10 a.m.	Cuinchy Defence Works - Kitchen Rd, revetting, drainage, & preparing for extension. New Rose trench - erecting parados. Widening & constructing barbed wire entanglement in front of Cuinchy/Village line. Continuing work on F.A, J & H Saps. Wolfe trench - fixing trench boards & cleaning trench. Greno Road - Cleaning and draining. M.G. emplacement No 1 cleaned out & made habitable. Overland track to Le Plantin, erecting screen obstructing horses & cellars in village line. Improving Windy Corner.	

WAR DIARY
INTELLIGENCE SUMMARY

(Erase heading not required.)

124th W. Coy. Roy. Royal Engineers

Army Form C. 2118.

Place	Date	Hour	Summary of Events and Information	Remarks and references to Appendices
73 d.4.4.	10.3.16	10 am	Same as for 9th. Clearing out drain from Scotch Trench to Boates Grange to take water from Scottish Trench & New Cut. Lumbering & enlarging T.M.B. dug-out.	
73 d.4.4.	11.3.16	10 am	Same as for 10th. Constructing M.G. emplacements at Snuck Farm & Givenchy Keep. 2nd Lieut. Bourgeois transferred to this Unit from New General Reserve.	
73 d.s.4.	12.3.16	10 am	Same as for 11th. Two dug-outs commence at Piccadilly. Drainage of Caledonian Rd, Hopper Cut, Stave Rd & Suez Canal in hand. Down St (New Trench) commenced.	
73 d.4.4.	13.3.16	10 am	Same as for 12th. Steel dug-out commenced at Piccadilly. Steel Shelter No.2 in Hamburg completed. Two sapping announced.	
73 d.4.4.	14.3.16	10 am	Same as for 13th.	
73 d.4.4.	15.3.16	10 am	Same as for 14th. Site for M.G. prepared at North Redoubt. Steel Shelter No.1 in Hamburg completed. Queens Rd - wiring of French Troops in hand. Enemy dropped few shells near billet.	
73 d.4.4.	16.3.16	10 am	Same as for 15th. Sap F & J through to Crater. Clearing drain in Sunken Rd. J Sap drained released.	
73 d.4.4.	17.3.16	10 am	Same as for 15th. Wave Rd open from Scottish Trench to New Cut. Artillery Rd in billet	
73 d.4.4.	18.3.16	10 am	Same as for 16th. Bench completed.	
73 d.4.4.	19.3.16	10 am	Same as 15th. Two Steel Shelters in Village line completed.	
73 d.4.s.	20.3.16	10 am	Same as 18th. Overland Track Complete to Le Martin South.	

WAR DIARY
INTELLIGENCE SUMMARY.
(Erase heading not required.)

Army Form C. 2118.

19th Field Coy Royal Engineers

Place	Date	Hour	Summary of Events and Information	Remarks and references to Appendices
73 d 4.4.	20.3.16	10 a.m.	Givenchy Defences. Mither Rd. Herts Avenue. - Revetting trench tranching & preparing for extension. New Cut - Clearing and relaying trench boards. Caledonian Rd - Wiring trench boards. Constructing dug-outs in Piccadilly & for T.M.B's. Near Ammn St - Contructing new trench. Duck Farm. - M.G. emplacement in hand. Givenchy Keep Herts Redoubt - Constructing M.G. emplacements. Le Plantin track completed for 420 yds. Village Line - 2 New Steel Shelters completed. Work continued on Northern part of Sapa.	
73 d 4.4.	21.3.16	10 a.m.	Same as 21st. Coldstream Rd Kings Road - Clearing out and drainage. Excavating old Communication trench at le Plantin. 220 yds boxes wiring completed Between Mitre Rd & the 3 M.G. 180 yds completed between Nos. 3 & 4 M.G. N Group Saps - 8 cross feet in galleries, such hole Exerces in H & J Saps. Erecting bomb shelter in new trench. Clearing & deepening H, I, J, & K Saps. 2nd Lieut. Bogart proceeded on leave to England, Ireland. Strong points in Givre Redoubt System & Trench line inspected and reported upon.	
73 d 4.4.	22.3.16	10 a.m.	Same as 22nd. 500 sq yds loose wiring completed between Canal & Windy Corner. Loose wiring continued between Windy Corner & Front M.G. 220 sq yds completed. & 150 yds wiring completed between Nos 5 & 6 M.G. Section front in Saps, & conducting connections between Saps. Two Sappers slightly wounded.	

W. Witchwood Major
OC 19th Field Coy R.E.

WAR DIARY

INTELLIGENCE SUMMARY

Army Form C. 2118.

Instructions regarding War Diaries and Intelligence Summaries are contained in F.S. Regs., Part II. and the Staff Manual respectively. Title pages will be prepared in manuscript.

(Erase heading not required.)

124th Field Coy. Royal Engineers

Place	Date	Hour	Summary of Events and Information	Remarks and references to Appendices
23 d.u.u.	24.3.16	10 a.m.	Same as 23rd. One Sapper wounded.	
23 d.u.u.	25.3.16	10 a.m.	Work in Bint owing to Brigade changing.	
23 d.u.u.	26.3.16	10 a.m.	Same as 23rd. Connection of Thomas Butts & Scottish trench commenced, approx. 60 x 3 wiring completed between Windy Corner & Port Fixe. 25 sq yards of 380.9 of b completed between No 2 & No. 6 M. Guns. Northern Group of Loop-hole Crows/put in.	
23 d.u.u.	27.3.16	10 a.m.	Same as 26th. O.P. for Infantry started at Trench Farm.	
23 d.u.u.	28.3.16	10 a.m.	Same as 26th. Site cleared for Battn. Headquarters, Dudorys Walk. M.G.emplacements at Trench Farm & Givenchy Keep cleared. Steel shelters in Village line completed. Revetting open M.G. emplacements. Village line, & repairing M.G. tables in emplacements.	
23 d.u.u.	29.3.16	10 a.m.	Same as 28th. Repairing pumps Village line.	
23 d.u.u.	30.3.16	10 a.m.	Same as 28th. Grenadier Road - revetting & laying trench boards.	
23 d.u.u.	31.3.16	10 a.m.	Same as 29th. Le Plantin track completed.	

J.R. Winterworth, Major R.E.
O.C. 124th Field Coy R.E.

WAR DIARY

INTELLIGENCE SUMMARY
(Erase heading not required.)

Army Form C. 2118.

XXXVIII

/24th Field Coy. Royal Engineers

Place	Date	Hour	Summary of Events and Information	Remarks and references to Appendices
23 d.v.4	1.4.16	10 am	Givenchy Defence work:- Wiring Vivage Line; revetting, laying trench boards & preparing for extension at Kitchen Road, Herts Avenue, Warr Road and Nut Cut. Gunacher Road (from jct with Grouse Butts to Front Line) Revetting and laying trench boards new Nouv St. Constructing new trench. Constructing two dug outs at Picadilly and one for T.M.B. Erection of Infantry O.P at Orchard Farm. Constructing roof for M.G emplacement at Herts Redoubt. Erecting steel shelters for Batten. Headquarters at Bird Cage Walk. - Northern Boat Saps - Driving saps, re-opening sap from J&K. sandbag revetment at various points.	
23 d.v.4	2.4.16	10 am	Same as for 1st.	
23 d.v.4	3.4.16	10 am	Same as for 1st. Repairing bridges of Vauxhall bridge – Birdcage Walk tramway ("H") Sap blown up. 2 Sappers & several infantry men killed. Relaying Vauxhall bridge to Birdcage Walk tramway.	
23 d.v.4	4.4.16	10 am	Same as for 3rd. New fire trench made from A.6 F. Sap. Superhet constructed in F. Sap. Re-opening H night hand Sap.	
23 d.v.4	5.4.16	10 am	Same as for 3rd. Right hand sap at A re-opened & edge of new crater. Improving new face of Front Line	
23 d.v.4	6.4.16	10 am	Same as for 4th. Wiring Vivage Line completed. Le Touret System. Posts repaired & moved.	

Army Form C. 2118.

WAR DIARY
INTELLIGENCE SUMMARY.
(Erase heads not required.)

1st/3rd Field Coy. Royal Engineers

Place	Date	Hour	Summary of Events and Information	Remarks and references to Appendices
23 d u 4	2/4/16	10 a.m.	Same as for 6th. Two dugouts constructed in Dealman's Trench.	
23 d u 4	8/4/16	10 a.m.	Same as for 6th. Recommenced to afs trench from J to K Sap.	
23 d u 4	9/4/16	10 a.m.	Same as for 8th. 2nd Lieut. Macquereymond Unit from leave.	
23 d u 4	10/4/16	10 a.m.	Same as for 8th. Removing old dug out in HSap. No working parties available owing to Brigade changing.	
23 d u 4	11/4/16	10 a.m.	Same as for 8th. Le Touret and Carre Becaro Systems - Posts inspected & reported on.	
23 d u 4	12/4/16	10 a.m.	Same as for 8th.	
23 d u 4	13/4/16	10 a.m.	Same as for 8th. One man killed & four men wounded in Sap working parties.	
23 d u 4	14/4/16	10 a.m.	Same as for 8th. Wiring in front Piccadilly.	
23 d u 4	15/4/16	10 a.m.	Same as for 14th. Widening and repeating new trench between H + I Saps.	
23 d u 4	16/4/16	10 a.m.	Same as for 15th. O.C. 23rd Field Coy. visited sites of various works with O.C. 1/3rd Infy.	
23 d u 4	17/4/16	10 a.m.	Handing over reports on positions & progress of works in hand and contemplated, particulars of R.E. Stores on hand and dealt with at Company Hindr, to O.C. 23rd Field Coy. R.E. Company moved at 9 a.m. to Estairs en route for Laventie.	
Estairs	18/4/16	10 a.m.	Company Billets at Estairs. Company moved at 10 a.m. for Laventie.	

Army Form C. 2118.

WAR DIARY
INTELLIGENCE SUMMARY.
(Erase heading not required.)

124th (Field Coy) Royal Engineers

Place	Date	Hour	Summary of Events and Information	Remarks and references to Appendices
Hog B.5.q	19.4.16	10 a.m.	Improving billets, erecting workshops etc.	
Hog B.5.q	20.4.16	10 a.m.	As for 19th. OC reffrews visited site of various works.	
Hog B.5.q	21.4.16	10 a.m.	As for 19th.	
Hog B.5.q	22.4.16	10 a.m.	Faverolle – Right Battn, Left Brigade area. Front line – Cleaning, relaying trench boards and raising fire steps. N.Elgin St, S.Elgin St, Meacolot St, Army Lane & Fleet St. Clearing fully, clearing trenches, relaying trench boards. Relaying Midland tramway. Improvements to second line. Evelin & OP's at The Peak & Chapigny, and improving billet. Repairs to ESqm. Road bend near Wangeroi Post.	
Hog B.5.q	23.4.16	10 a.m.	As for 22nd. OP at Chapigny chimney completed. Erecting bomb store at Banquisart Post. Constructing reserve trench (300 yd line).	
Hog B.5.q	24.4.16	10 a.m.	As for 23rd.	
Hog B.5.q	25.4.16	10 a.m.	As for 23rd. Chapigny (Arrington Park) OP. completed.	
Hog B.5.q	26.4.16	11 a.m.	As for 23rd. Major Kirkwood proceeded to Boulogne. Company under command of Lieut. J. McMurtrie R.E. during Major Kirkwood's absence.	
Hog B.5.q	27.4.16	10 a.m.	As for 23rd. Complete plate to new hole faced in Lin's Farm Pt. Bomb store completed in Banquisart Post. Survey made & plans prepared for the guard of the OP. First run of workshop huts up nearly [completed]	

Army Form C. 2118.

WAR DIARY
INTELLIGENCE SUMMARY.
(Erase heading not required.)

134th (West Humphrey) Royal Engineers

Place	Date	Hour	Summary of Events and Information	Remarks and references to Appendices
Hog b-5.9	28.4.16	10am	As for 23rd – Constructing Cable & strengthening roofs of No1 M.G. emplacement & constructing dug-out in front line. Overhead steel cover window constructed in Min O.P. – Starting of carrier of Chateau Redoubt O.P.	
Hog b-5.9	29.4.16	10am	As for 28th – Repairs to No 2 M.G. emplacement & parados, front line.	
b.9 b.59	30.4.16	10am	As for 29th – Survey made & plans prepared for O.P.'s at Cm Farm & Winter Grange. One man of working party wounded.	

J W McIntire
Lieut R.E.
for Major R.E.
O.C. 134th (W) Field Coy. R.E.

WAR DIARY
INTELLIGENCE SUMMARY
(Erase heading not required.)

Army Form C. 2118.

XXVII (a) Field Coy Royal Engineers Vol 6

Instructions regarding War Diaries and Intelligence Summaries are contained in F.S. Regs., Part II. and the Staff Manual respectively. Title pages will be prepared in manuscript.

Place	Date	Hour	Summary of Events and Information	Remarks and references to Appendices
Map b5.9	1/5/16	10am	Laventie Area — Relaying Mustard Rly. Cleaning and wiring Macolot St, N. Elgin St, S. Elgin St, Robot St, Reaui Avenue, Shury Lane. Constructing two M.G. emplacements at Macolot Post. Erection of Rear and Dead Cow Artillery O.P.'s. Front line — Erecting wire other, refixing trench boards, repairs to parapet, parados, & M.G. emplacements.	
Map b5.9	2/5/16	10am	Same as for 1st. — Erecting wire entanglement, Bridgeabrie.	
Map b5.9	3/5/16	10am	Do for 2nd.	
Map b5.9	4/5/16	10am	Do for 2nd. One man killed & 9 or wounded from working party. Cutting & planting trees ready for screening Rue Tilleloy. 2nd Lieut Savages wounded on leave England.	
Map b5.9	5/5/16	10am	Do for 4th.	
Map b5.9	6/5/16	10am	Do for 4th. — Do for One NCO & two Sappers slightly wounded	
Map b5.9	7/5/16	10am	Do for 4th. One man & working party wounded	
Map b5.9	8/5/16	10am	Do for 4th.	
Map b5.9	9/5/16	10am	Do for 4th.	
Map b5.9	10/5/16	10am	Do for 4th.	

WAR DIARY
INTELLIGENCE SUMMARY

124th Field Coy. Royal Engineers

Army Form C. 2118.

Place	Date	Hour	Summary of Events and Information	Remarks and references to Appendices
No 9	11.5.16	10am	Tourquinant Section – Erection of O.P.s at The Peak, Erith Crescent. Constructing new trench. Relaying Midland tramway. Cleaning, repairing & resetting Maxelot Comn trench. Constructing two M.G. emplacements at Maxelot Post. Wiring Buckqrant line, screening Rue Suleby, erecting fire steps, relaying trench boards, repair to parapet and parados of front line. Cleaning revetting. N. Elgin St., S. Elgin St., Maxelot St., Albany Lane. O.C. returned from Boulogne.	
No 9 B. S. 9	12.5.16	10am	Same as for 11th.	
No 9 A. S. 9	13.5.16	10am	As for 11th. Erection of Mortal Change O.P. commenced	
No 9 B. S. 9	14.5.16	10am	As for 13th.	
No 9 B. S. 9	15.5.16	10am	As for 13th.	
No 9 B. S. 9	16.5.16	10am	As for 13th. Screening of Road End commenced. Constructs bridge on Maxelot emergency road.	
No 9 B. S. 9	17.5.16	10am	As for 15th. Transport inspected by A.D.O.S. Major Parkment provides telephones in bore.	
No 9 L. S. 9	18.5.16	10am	As for 15th.	
No 9 B. S. 9	19.5.16	10am	As for 15th.	
No 9 B. S. 9	20.5.16	10am	As for 15th. New loop hole first in Chaplogny O.P.	

Army Form C. 2118.

WAR DIARY
INTELLIGENCE SUMMARY
(Erase heading not required.)

1st Field Coy Royal Engineers

Place	Date	Hour	Summary of Events and Information	Remarks and references to Appendices
Map 65 q	21.5.16	10 am	Transport section — Erection of O.P.'s at Neuville Circuit, Moats Grange, Mun OP, Reas OP. Revetting and sandbagging S. Elgin, N. Elgin, Macelot, Kings Cave communication trenches. Front Line — Construction of Reserve Dugouts. T.M. emplacements & M.G. emplacements. Leaving job between Wangers and Road Bend Posts. Wiring Bacquerot Line, constructing M.G. emplacements at Moncelet Post, deepening & revetting Moncelet Communication Trench. Construction of Reserve Trench. Relaying Macland Tramway.	
Map 65 q	22.5.16	10 am	As for 21st. Reserve Dugouts in Front Line completed. 2nd Lieut Maguire wounded.	
Map 65 q	23.5.16	10 am	As for 21st	
Map 65 q	24.5.16	10 am	As for 21st	
Map 65 q	25.5.16	10 am	As for 21st. Leaving job between Wangers and Road Bend Posts completed. 2nd Kent Coy joins line. Erection of Advanced Brigade Headquarters commenced. Sentry shelter in front line.	
Map 65 q	26.5.16	10 am	As for 25th	
Map 65 q	27.5.16	10 am	As for 25th. 2nd Lieut. F.P. Oehler joined Company vice 2nd Lieut Maguire.	
Map 65 q	28.5.16	10 am	As for 27th	
Map 65 q	29.5.16	10 am	As for 27th. 2nd Lieut Grogan proceeded England on leave.	
Map 65 q	30.5.16	10 am	As for 27th	
Map 65 q	31.5.16	10 am	As for 27th. Sentry shelter in front line completed. Commenced excavation.	

WAR DIARY

INTELLIGENCE SUMMARY

124th Field Coy R.E.

Army Form C. 2118.

Place	Date	Hour	Summary of Events and Information	Remarks and references to Appendices
Hq Rt. 9	4/5/16 (Continued)	10 am	for three steel shelters in support line. One section of 1/3 South Midland R.E.T. attached to this Unit for instruction.	

Jno Murtrie
Lieut. R.E.
for O.C. 124th Field Coy R.E.

WAR DIARY
or
INTELLIGENCE SUMMARY

JUNE 38/ Army Form C. 2118.
124th Field Coy. R.E. Vol

Place	Date	Hour	Summary of Events and Information	Remarks and references to Appendices
M.9.6.59	1-6-16	10 a.m	Lavanto Area. — Tanguisart Section. — Relaying Midland tramway, Clearing, Deepening & revetting Maxelot Comm. Trench. Erection of O.P's at the Peak, Mine O.P. Castle bivouacs, Montes Grange. Revetting and bagging S. Elgin, N. Elgin, Maxelot, Drury Lane Comm. trenches. Construction of Reserve line. Front line. Construction of Reserve depôt, T.M. Emplacements to M.G. emplacements. Wiring Bacquart Line. Constructing M.G. emplacements at Maxelot Pot. Erection of Advanced Brigade Headquarters, excavation for steel shelters in support line.	
			Two men of working party wounded.	
M.9.6.59	2.6.16	10 a.m	As for 1st.	
M.9.6.59	3.6.16	10 a.m	As for 1st. 1 N.C.O. slightly wounded + 2 men of working party wounded.	
M.9.6.59	4.6.16	10 a.m	As for 1st. Laying pipe track for water supply Bacquart St. 2nd Lt. Maguire rejoins unit from hospital. Illus. Battn. Headquarters. Work commenced. Excavating	
M.9.6.59	5.6.16		As for 4th. Wiring 6 right of Maxelot Trench. C.T.S. of Tanguisart Post being repaired	
M.9.6.59	6.6.16		As for 5th. No working parties available owing to Brigade changing. 2nd Lt. M.T. Cooper rejoins Unit from leave.	

WAR DIARY
or
INTELLIGENCE SUMMARY

Army Form C. 2118.

(Erase heading not required.)

12th Field Coy. R.E.

Instructions regarding War Diaries and Intelligence Summaries are contained in F. S. Regs., Part II. and the Staff Manual respectively. Title pages will be prepared in manuscript.

Place	Date	Hour	Summary of Events and Information	Remarks and references to Appendices
M.q.b.5.q.	7.6.16	10 a.m.	As for 5th. Lieut. McMartin proceeds on leave. 2nd/Lieut. M. Cooper assumes command of the Company.	
M.q.b.5.q.	8.6.16	10 a.m.	As for 5th. New trench dug at Red Lamp Salient from N.13.a.6.1. to N.13.b.6.6t.3. a distance of 250yards. A communication trench was made 80 yards long in centre of new trench. Wire entanglement half complete. Working party 250. Covering party 50. Supper 20. 2nd/Lts. Cooper, Davies, Potter, Maguire.	
M.q.b.5.q.	9.6.16	10 a.m.	As for 8th. I Sapper wounded. 2nd/Lt. Horgan rejoins Unit from leave.	
M.q.b.5.q.	10.6.16	10 a.m.	Handing over reports on positions & progress of works in hand. Particulars of R.E. Stores on hand at Ecoivres Dump & Trench Stores &c. O.C. 2/2 South Midland R.E. T.F. Company moved at 12·30 p.m. to Bruay.	
P.31.C.4.0	11.6.16	10 a.m.	Cleaning, washing togans etc. Improving billets.	
	12.6.16	10 a.m.	As for 11th.	
	13.6.16	10 a.m.	Company moved from Bruay to Auchel at 10 a.m.	
Auchel	14.6.16	10 a.m.	Left Auchel for Villers Bretan at 9 a.m.	
Villers Bretan	15.6.16	10 a.m.	Technical training & improving billets.	

Army Form C. 2118.

WAR DIARY
INTELLIGENCE SUMMARY.
(Erase heading not required.)

13th Field Coy. Royal Engineers

Place	Date	Hour	Summary of Events and Information	Remarks and references to Appendices
Hillers Bruli	16.6.16	10am	Technical Training	
"	17.6.16	10am	Ditto	
"	18.6.16	10am	Ditto	
"	19.6.16	10am	Holiday. Major Kirkwood Lieut McMurtrie rejoined Coy from leave.	
"	20.6.16	10am	Technical Training	
"	21.6.16	10am	Ditto	
"	22.6.16	10am	Ditto	
"	23.6.16	10am	Ditto	
"	24.6.16	10am	Brigade Training out 1st Brigade	
"	25.6.16	10am	Divisional Training out 38th Div.	
"	26.6.16	10am	Company marched from Villers Bretan to Rancourt	
Rancourt	27.6.16	10am	" — Rancourt to Epicamps	
Epicamps	28.6.16	10am	Resting.	
"	29.6.16	10am	Improving billets &c	
"	30.6.16	10am	Company left Epicamps for Val de Maison. J.M. Kirkwood Major R.E. O.C. 13th Field Coy R.E.	

2353 Wt. W2344/1454 700,000 5/15 D. D. & L. A.D.S.S./Forms/C. 2118.

Secret

Original War Diary.
September 1917.

124th Field Coy. Royal Engineers
38th Welsh Division

CONFIDENTIAL.

WAR DIARY

of

124th Field Company R.E.

38th (Welsh) Division

July. 1916.

WAR DIARY
or
INTELLIGENCE SUMMARY.
(Erase heading not required.)

124th Field Coy Royal Engineers

Army Form C. 2118.

Place	Date	Hour	Summary of Events and Information	Remarks and references to Appendices
Val de Maison	1.7.16	8.0 a.m.	Company marched from Val de Maison to Lealincourt.	
Lealincourt	2.7.16	10.0 a.m.	Waiting orders	
do	3.7.16	10.0 a.m.	Company marched from Lealincourt to Henencourt l'Abbé.	
Henencourt l'Abbé	4.7.16	10.0 a.m.	Waiting orders at Henencourt l'Abbé.	
do	5.7.16	10.0 a.m.	Company marched to Minden Post. N° Maneys (Sgt. W.M. Workshop n.p.) & Bivouaced for night. N°s 1 & 2 sections out - to Strong Then QUADRANGLE TRENCH.	
Minden Post Mametz	6.7.16	10.0 a.m.	Company "standing to" in readiness to proceed to Mametz Wood.	
do	7.7.16	"	Company proceeded to half Support under orders to proceed to Mametz Wood 1,2 & 3 Sections dispatched orders in QUEENS NULLAH from G.O.C. 113th Bde to Construct Strong Point at Entrance to Mametz Wd. 9 am. Same as 7th. Area reconnoitred with G.O.C. 113th Bde. returned to Minden Post 6.30 a.m.	
Half Support	8.7.16	10.0 a.m.	Bivouac at Half Sunt shelled by enemy, killing one driver. Company returned to bivouac at Minden Post.	
do	9.7.16	10.0 a.m.	Operations for attack on Mametz Wood. One section of Unit took up position in rear of Bartzy Alley at 5 a.m. and one took up position in same Nullah at the same time. At 5.45 a.m. Southern portion of wood was reported clear of enemy. 1 Lieut Compton was instructed to reconnoitre the wood & find out the exact position of affairs. He did this, and proceeded with his section at 7.15 a.m. and left for QUEENS to construct strong point at junction of Wood trench & Strip trench.	
Minden Post	10.7.16	10.0 a.m.		

Army Form C. 2118.

WAR DIARY
or
INTELLIGENCE SUMMARY.
(Erase heading not required.)

17th Field Coy. Royal Engineers

Place	Date	Hour	Summary of Events and Information	Remarks and references to Appendices
Maricourt Wood	10/7/16	Cont.	At 5.45am the remaining two sections advanced from behind Dangic Alley to the positions at Queens Redoubt, entered the wood at 7.45am and proceeded to construct the strong point at first cross roads in Central Avenue. At 9am in finding the Infantry were not making sufficient progress in consolidating the taken st., O.C. 98th Div. Pioneers from communication trenches put them on consolidating new line. O.C. was delayed in reconnaissance of wood by being put in charge of left flank of attack by Brig General Candy 113th Brigade, there being no Infantry Officers available. At 4pm Engineers Pioneers had to man the new trench to enable Infantry to advance to clear remaining part of wood, occupying two lines of our line. At 6.15pm Infantry proceeded to make final sweep of woods, and at 9pm they retired on to Central strong point at the cross roads, where they were started up by RE's who manned this point. Infantry Pioneers start to clearing remaining part of night. The casualties of Unit on this date were – One Officer wounded, One Sapper killed, 3 NCO's wounded, 16 Sappers wounded.	

J.W. Richardson Major RE

WAR DIARY

INTELLIGENCE SUMMARY.

Army Form C. 2118.

(Erase heading not required.) 1 Sep W? recd by Royal Engineers

Place	Date	Hour	Summary of Events and Information	Remarks and references to Appendices
Mametz Wood	11.7.16		Constructing strong points on Western flank of Wood, at junction of bottom edge of Wood roadway, also at junction of front support trench with wood. also construction of new front line. Casualties – 2 Officers wounded. 3 O.R. killed 16 O.R. wounded 30 O.R. missing.	
Y.17.b.	12.7.16 10am	Company withdrawn from Bazentin Wood – been during night of 11th-12th July relieved by 7th Division – bivouaced during day, leaving for MEAULTE at 5pm. Company bivouaced at MEAULTE during night of 12 & 13th July & left at 3am for Ribemont.	
Ribemont Sailly au Bois	13.7.16			
	14.7.16 10am	Company marched from Ribemont to Sailly au Bois.	
	15.7.16 10am	Reconnaissance of Hebuterne area by Officers, 1st of Field by South Midland R.E.'s. T.F. No. 3 sector billets in Hebuterne then being re-equipped.	
"	16.7.16 noon	Hebuterne area:- O.C. examined work required to be done with Brigadier. Construction of dug-outs in Hebuterne Village & improving bivouac.	
"	17.7.16 noon	Hebuterne area:- Repairing of Ancestrale, No. 20, Sear Bart, Nairn commenced. Construction of dugouts continued – Laying new fire trench in front line from K19a38 & K23a52 (Hebuterne map). 1 Lieut. A.D. Banks & 2 other ranks wounded. 11 Lieuts. A.S. Banks & La Clock joined company	W.R.W. wildwire telegraph

WAR DIARY or INTELLIGENCE SUMMARY

Army Form C. 2118.

Place	Date	Hour	Summary of Events and Information	Remarks and references to Appendices
Indian Div	18/7/16	10am	**Vermelles Area** – Repairing of Annextall No.110, Jean Bart + Maine Continued. Construction of dug outs and erection of R.A.M.C. dressing station in Vermelles village continued. Reconnaissance of area with new officer, Lt. seconded work with Brig. General Cmdg 1st Brigade.	1st Field Coy Royal Engineers
do	19.7.16	10am	Same work as for 18th.	
do	20.7.16	10am	As for 19th. Working to left of Rue de Vir on original front line. Erection of Sand bag screens to protect water tank and engine at Valentine. Also clearing original front line to left of Jean Bart St.	
do	21.7.16	10am	Annextall – Rigging sumps for drainage. No 140 Cutting out fire step, Jean Bart, Relaying trench boards & clearing sump. Clearing front line trench from Rue de Vir to Valentine & laying trench boards. digging out communication trench between end of Saint Amour & Vermelles trench, also between Rue of Saint Amour & end of dressing station. Construction of dug outs & dressing station continued. Clearing Jean Bart, Kerr St.,	Withdrawn sheets
do	22.7.16	10am	As for 21st instant.	
do	23.7.16	10am	As for 22nd. 2nd Lieut. A. Cooper joined Company.	

Army Form C. 2118.

WAR DIARY
INTELLIGENCE SUMMARY
(Erase heading not required.)

Instructions regarding War Diaries and Intelligence Summaries are contained in F.S. Regs., Part II. and the Staff Manual respectively. Title pages will be prepared in manuscript.

134th Field Coy. Royal Engineers

Place	Date	Hour	Summary of Events and Information	Remarks and references to Appendices
Sailly au Bois	26/7/16	10 am	Nebutune Area – Front trench improvement – Cutting new trench through to front line, improving front line N of Knox & between Luce & Lit. Clearing pas de tir, widening & deepening Third Lane, & Protest. Clearing, deepening & constructing fire steps in Eastern d' Auchope, construction of strong point at jct of Knox & Jena. Clearing & erecting fire steps in Jean Bart. Deepening Northern Communication trench to New trench AA. Clearing & deepening Knott communication trench. Demingen – Clearing & constructing strong trench. Chisell – Clearing. Construction of New trench "AA". Construction of dug outs & RAMC Dressing Station in Hebuterne Village.	
do	27/7/16	10 am	do do do	
do	28/7/16	10 am	do do do	
do	29/7/16	10 am	do do do	
do	30/7/16	10 am	Hebuterne area handed over to 132nd Field Coy R.E. Company marched from Sailly au Bois to St Leger les Authie & bivouaced at same place.	
St Leger les Authie	31/7/16	10 am	Drill.	
do	30/7/16	6 am	Coy marched from St Leger les Authie to Authicule & bivouaced at latter place.	Milward Major

Army Form C. 2118.

WAR DIARY
or
INTELLIGENCE SUMMARY.
(Erase heading not required.)

124th Field Coy Royal Engineers

Place	Date	Hour	Summary of Events and Information	Remarks and references to Appendices
Authierle	31-7-16		Coy. marched from Authierle to Mollens, entrained at Mollens, detrained at Argues, & then marched to Volkerinckhove.	

R.R. Kirkwood Major R.E.
O.C. 124 Field Coy R.E.

2353 Wt. W2544/1454 700,000 5/15 D. D. & L. A.D.S.S./Forms/C.2118.

Confidential (original)

War Diary
of
124th Field Company,
Royal Engineers
38th (Welsh) Division

August 1916.

Army Form C. 2118.

WAR DIARY
INTELLIGENCE SUMMARY.
(Erase heading not required.)

[2nd/1st Lowland Coy. Royal Engineers]

Place	Date	Hour	Summary of Events and Information	Remarks and references to Appendices
Volkerinckhove	1.8.16	10am	Technical training, improvement of Billet, and construction of Rifle training School.	
	2.8.16	10am	As for 1st.	
	3.8.16	10am	Company marched from Volkerinckhove to Wormhoudt.	
Wormhoudt	4.8.16	10am	Company conveyed by lorries from Wormhoudt to Elverdinghe. Unit attached to VIIIth Corps for work on Elverdinghe Defences. Improving billets.	
Elverdinghe	5.8.16	10am	Construction of dug outs & M.G. emplacements, re-opening trenches for improving Elverdinghe Defences. "2" Line inspected & reports prepared for VIIIth Corps.	
do	6.8.16	10am	Work on Elverdinghe Defences continued.	
do	7.8.16	10am	Clearing Communication Trenches & cellars. Opening out brickwork and boring out for M.G. emplacements. Strengthening cellars. Constructing Strong Points. M.G. emplacements and dug outs.	
do	8.8.16	10am	As for 7th.	
do	9.8.16	10am	As for 8th. "X" Line reconnoitred by O.C. & reported on. Sandbagging windows etc. at Chateau. Gas alarm at 10.30pm.	
do	10.8.16	10am	As for 7th.	

WAR DIARY

INTELLIGENCE SUMMARY.

(Erase heading not required.)

Army Form C. 2118.

Instructions regarding War Diaries and Intelligence Summaries are contained in F.S. Regs., Part II. and the Staff Manual respectively. Title pages will be prepared in manuscript.

1st Field Coy. Royal Engineers

Place	Date	Hour	Summary of Events and Information	Remarks and references to Appendices
Elverdinghe	11.8.16	10 a.m.	Elverdinghe Defences – Constructing new strong points, M.G. emplacements, new shelter trenches. Clearing trenches. Enlarging cellars and ground floor Dy. Chateau.	
do	12.8.16	10 a.m.	As for 11th. Wiring, revetting, erecting bullet proofs parados, fire step at "L2" strong point.	
do	13.8.16	10 a.m.	As for 12th. Officers of Cyclist Batt. shown work reported on "X" line.	
do	14.8.16	10 a.m.	Men resting. Clearing billets &c.	
do	15.8.16	10 a.m.	As for 12th. Work of strengthening "X" line continued.	
do	16.8.16	10 a.m.	As for 15th. Rec'd Sgt. 14 Brigade round Elverdinghe defences. Inspected "L2". Stoke & cut features for accommodation of 400 men in Boesinghe.	
do	17.8.16	10 a.m.	As for 15th. Clearing sites for new dugouts in Chateau grounds. Bullet shells commenced. "I.N.G." & "B" type.	
do	18.8.16	10 a.m.	do do do. Revetting trenches at "X" line & construction of dug outs continued in Chateau.	
do	19.8.16	10 a.m.	As for 18th.	
do	20.8.16	10 a.m.	As for 18th.	
do	21.8.16	10 a.m.	Three sections proceeded to C.1.9.C.3.3 (Sheet 28 N.W.) and took over work from 1st Northern & 11th Siege M.E. Lieut. Vancouver joined Company. The alarm at E. 30 for. and 10.35 p.m.	

Army Form C. 2118.

WAR DIARY
INTELLIGENCE SUMMARY.
(Erase heading not required.)

1st Field Coy. Royal Engineers

Instructions regarding War Diaries and Intelligence Summaries are contained in F. S. Regs., Part II. and the Staff Manual respectively. Title pages will be prepared in manuscript.

Place	Date	Hour	Summary of Events and Information	Remarks and references to Appendices
(Ref 28NW) C.19.C.3.3	21.8.16 (Con.td)	10pm	No. 3 Section remained at Elverdinghe to carry on work on Elverdinghe Defences. "Fins" & dug outs in Chateau Grounds.	
C.19.C.3.3	22.8.16	10am	Left Sector, Ypres salient – Clearing drains, deepening new front between C.13.a.88.16 C.13.b.08. Constructing dug out for O.P. Relaying trench boards & improving drainage of Canadian Trench. Construction of forward dug outs on Fargate Strong Point. Hunt Shipton strong point. Erecting bridge room on Yprès twist. Canal bridges regularly patrolled and necessary repairs effected. No. 3 Section continued work on Elverdinghe Defences, dug outs in Chateau grounds, and improvements of "L2" and "X" lines.	
do	23.8.16	10am	As for 22nd. Headqrs. Section & transport took over transport lines returns from 1st Renfrew Field Coy. R.E.	
do	24.8.16	10pm	As for 22nd. 1 Driver tpfer to Hospital	
do	25.8.16	10am	As for 22nd.	
do	26.8.16	10am	As for 22nd.	
do	27.8.16	10am	As for 22nd.	1 Sapper to Hospital
do	28.8.16	10am	As for 22nd.	1 O/Rank to hosp. Joined Coy.

Army Form C. 2118.

WAR DIARY

~~INTELLIGENCE~~ SUMMARY.

121st Field Coy. R.E.

(Erase heading not required.)

Instructions regarding War Diaries and Intelligence Summaries are contained in F. S. Regs. Part II. and the Staff Manual respectively. Title pages will be prepared in manuscript.

Place	Date	Hour	Summary of Events and Information	Remarks and references to Appendices
Ypres N.W. C.19.C.3.3	29/8/16	10am	Left Sector - Ypres Salient - Clearing drains, Construction of Dugouts, Construction of Targets, Rushpion Strong Points Continued. Erection of bridge & screen over Yperlee continued. Cross bridges regularly patrolled & necessary repairs effected. No 3 Section continued work on Blauwbrugge Defences, dug outs in Chateau grounds, and improvement of by and X trico. See also 4pm. Lieut McMurtrie reported Company.	
do	30/8/16	10am	Do for 29th.	
do	31/8/16	10am	Do for 29th.	

J. McMurtrie Lt. for Major R.E.
O.C. 121st Field Coy. R.E.

Vol 10

War Diary
12th Field Coy. R.E.
September 1916

Army Form C. 2118.

WAR DIARY
INTELLIGENCE SUMMARY
(Erase heading not required.)

2nd/1st Field Coy Royal Engineers

Place	Date	Hour	Summary of Events and Information	Remarks and references to Appendices
(Sheet 28 NW)				
C.19.C.3.3	1.9.16	10am	Left Sector, Ypres Salient. Nos. 1. 2 & 4 Sections employed on clearing drains, construction of dugouts, Targets and Skipton Strong Points, erection of Lady screen over Ypres. Patrolling & repairing Canal Bridges. No. 3 Section continued work on Elverdinghe Defences, dug outs in Elverdinghe Chateau grounds, and improvement of "h2" & "h" line Elverdinghe Chateau grounds, and improvement of "h2" & "h" line Elverdinghe Defences, dug outs. (Lieut McMurtrie on Court of Enquiry into cause of fire at 126th Brigade R.F.A.)	
C.19.C.33	2.9.16	10am	do for 1d.	
C.19.C.33	3.9.16	10am	do for 1d.	
C.19.C.33	4.9.16	9:30am	do for 1d. (Absentee men's gas helmets inspected by Lieut McMurtrie).	
C.19.C.33	5.9.16	10am	do for 1d.	
do	6.9.16	10am	do for 1d.	
do	7.9.16	10am	do for 1d.	
do	7.9.16	10am	do for 1d.	
do	8.9.16	10am	do for 1d.	
do	9.9.16	9:30am	do for 1d.	
do	10.9.16	10am	do for 1d. With exception that work on Elverdinghe Defences, dug outs.	

Army Form C. 2118.

WAR DIARY
or
INTELLIGENCE SUMMARY.
(Erase heading not required.)

1/2 H Field Coy. RE

Instructions regarding War Diaries and Intelligence Summaries are contained in F.S. Regs., Part II. and the Staff Manual respectively. Title pages will be prepared in manuscript.

Place	Date	Hour	Summary of Events and Information	Remarks and references to Appendices
(Sheet 28 NW) C19 C.3.3	10.9.16	10 am	N° Line and L-5 work handed over to 9th Field Coy RE., and N° 2 Section joined Company on Canal Bank.	
do	11.9.16	6 pm	Left Sector – Ypres Salient :– Clearing drains, construction of Targets, dug-outs, Targets Redifts, Strong points, dug outs on Canal Bank, patrolling & repairing Canal Bridges. (Sgt Duncanson transferred to 99 Field Drainage Coy.)	
do	12.9.16	"	Light Spring J wagon sent to Abbeville.	
do	13.9.16	9.16 pm	do for 11th	
do	14.9.16	9.16 pm	do for 11th Construction of Strong Signallers Dugout commenced and repairs to Tramway.	
do	15.9.16	10 am	do for 11th	
do	16.9.16	" pm	do for 11th	
do	17.9.16	10 am	do for 11th	
do	18.9.16	10 pm	do for 11th Cooper, Lance Corporal promoted to Corporal Sergeant.	
do	19.9.16	10 am	do for 11th	
do	20.9.16	9.16 pm	do for 11th	
do	21.9.16	10 am	do for 11th N° 4 Section proceeded to Rest Billets at A15 b 88. (Sheet 28 NW)	

WAR DIARY
or
INTELLIGENCE SUMMARY

(Erase heading not required.) By Major A.V. Royal Engineers

Army Form C. 2118.

Place	Date	Hour	Summary of Events and Information	Remarks and references to Appendices
(Auvergne) C.19.C.3.3	22.9.16	10 am	Left sector:- Ypres Salient :- Work on Langest Strongpoint, Langest Res. trench Canal bank trench continued. Patrolling & repairing Canal Bridges & tramways continued. Construction of dug outs, Gun boat etc. & strong dugouts dug out on Ypres Bank proceed with. Work on Skipton Post continued. No. 4 section in rest billet making new horse lines. Rest of No. 4 sec. respirators issued to No.1,2,3 sections. New entanglements in front of Support Front line removed reported on. Survey made of enfiladed strong point at B12 A57½.	
do	23.9.16	10 am	Work as for 22nd continued. Dismantling 3 bays of bridge 6. Men at Rest Billet unvaccinated. 3 Caie dump joined Company.	
do	24.9.16	10 am	Work as for 22nd – also new floating piers & trestle & superstructure reconstructed on bridge 6. Major Kirkwood proceeded on leave to England. Three personnel consigned upon withdrawal of 100 lb H.T. shelters & H.E. shell.	
do	25.9.16	10 am	Work as for 22nd – No 4 section employed on ensuring works in "back" area. Box respirators issued to that section between 2E.	
do	26.9.16	10 am	Work as for 25th.	
do	27.9.16	10 am	Work as for 25th.	

Army Form C. 2118.

(IV)

WAR DIARY
INTELLIGENCE SUMMARY.
(Erase heading not required.)

125th Field Coy. Royal Engineers

Instructions regarding War Diaries and Intelligence Summaries are contained in F. S. Regs., Part II. and the Staff Manual respectively. Title pages will be prepared in manuscript.

Place	Date	Hour	Summary of Events and Information	Remarks and references to Appendices
Ypres (NW) C.10.C.33.&.9.Ypres				
do	29.9.16	9pm	Left Sector :- Ypres Salient :- Work as for 25th. Work as for 25th. Commenced work on front line with No. 3 Section, strengthening parapet, pinning down fire trench and putting in RE truck at E.23, E.25, E.25 & R.1a.b. Enemy trench mortar ponfile prevented our troops to England.	
do	30.9.16	10am	Work as 29th continued	
do	1.10.16	10am	do	

J.M.Murtrin
Lieut. R.E. for Major R.E.
O.C. 125th Field Coy R.E.
by J.M.

Secret VOLII   Confidential

Original
War Diary - October - 1916.
_____

124 Field Coy. R.E.   38th (Welsh) Divn.
_____

31-10-16.

… Army Form C. 2118.

WAR DIARY
INTELLIGENCE SUMMARY.
(Erase heading not required.)

12th Field Coy. Royal Engineers

Place	Date	Hour	Summary of Events and Information	Remarks and references to Appendices
Map Sheet 28.N.W. C.19.C.3.3	1.10.16	10am	Left Sector:- Work on Bargate Dugouts and Strong Point, also new tracks. Pitching & repairing bridges over Canal, repair section of tramways. Construction of Gun Posts & Strong Signallers' dug out, & other dug outs in Yorks and Canal Banks. Constructing new trenches and dugouts in frontline. Work on Shipton Post continued. No. 4 Section in rest billets employed on horse standings, anthrax laundry etc.	
	2.10.16	9am	As for 1st.	
	3.10.16	9am	As for 1st.	
	4.10.16	10am	As for 1st. No 2 Section moved to rest billet & took over No.4 Section Work. No 4 Section moved to Canal Bank & took over No 2 Section Work.	
	5.10.16	9am	Work as for 1st.	
	6.10.16	9am	Ditto. Major Kirkwood returned from leave. Lieut Smethwick wounded.	
	7.10.16	9am	Ditto.	
	8.10.16	9am	Ditto. Capt Brunwood R.E, 2nd Army Central School attached for instruction.	
	9.10.16	9am	Ditto.	
	10.10.16	9am	Ditto. 2 Lieut L.N. Barrett joined Coy. 2 Lieut E.O. Mason admitted to Hospital.	

Army Form C. 2118.

WAR DIARY
or
INTELLIGENCE SUMMARY.
(Erase heading not required.)

124th Field Coy. Royal Engineers

Instructions regarding War Diaries and Intelligence Summaries are contained in F.S. Regs., Part II. and the Staff Manual respectively. Title pages will be prepared in manuscript.

Place	Date	Hour	Summary of Events and Information	Remarks and references to Appendices
Sht N.19 28 C.19 C.33	10.10.16	10.a.m.	Two Officers & 100 O.R. from 118 Infantry Brigade attached to Coy. for permanent working parties.	Daily readings Ypres-Strate and Ypres-Canal de Sypres	Canal de L'yser
	11.10.16	10 a.m.	Work as for 10th		
	12.10.16	10 a.m.	ditto		
	13.10.16	10 a.m.	ditto		10"
	14.10.16	10 a.m.	ditto		11"
	15.10.16	10 a.m.	ditto	10"	11"
	16.10.16	10 a.m.	Capt. Greenwood R.E. left & report General Army Central School	11"	1' 0"
	17.10.16	10 a.m.	ditto	1' 0"	1' 1"
	18.10.16	10 a.m.	No. 1 Section proceeded Khai Built, rechanged work rebuilt with No.2 Section	1' 2"	1' 3"
	19.10.16	10 a.m.	ditto	1' 5"	1' 7"
	20.10.16	10 a.m.	ditto	1' 6"	3' 3"
	21.10.16	10 a.m.	ditto Lieut Anson returned from Hospital	1' 4"	3' 0"
	22.10.16	10 a.m.	ditto	1' 2"	3' 0"
	23.10.16	10 a.m.	ditto Gas alarm at 7.25 p.m.	1' 0"	2' 5"
	24.10.16	10 a.m.	ditto	1' 0"	1' 1"

Army Form C. 2118.

WAR DIARY
or
INTELLIGENCE SUMMARY.
(Erase heading not required.)

VI 124th Field Coy Royal Engineers

Instructions regarding War Diaries and Intelligence Summaries are contained in F.S. Regs., Part II. and the Staff Manual respectively. Title pages will be prepared in manuscript.

Place	Date	Hour	Summary of Events and Information	Remarks and references to Appendices
Rue NH 28				Daily readings of water level gauges
C.19.C.3.3.	25.10.16	10.a.m.	Left Sector - Ypres Salient. Work on Targets Strong Point, Argents, Machine Trenches continued. Latrines & repairing Canal Bridges. Repairing watching trenches. Construction of Gun Hut Pens, Strong Signallers Dugout & bullet dugouts on Yorks & Lancs Banks continued. Constructing New Trenches & dug outs in Support Line. Work on Skipton Rd continued. No. 1 Section employed on Stoke in lock area.	YPERLEE. CANAL de L'YSER. 11" 1' 1"
	26.10.16	10.am	As for 25th.	1" 0" 2' 0"
	27.10.16	10.am	do.	11" 2' 0"
	28.10.16	10.am	do.	11" 2' 1"
	29.10.16	10.am	do.	11" 2' 1"
	30.10.16	10.am	do.	12" 2' 0"
	31.10.16	10.am	do.	13" 2' 1"
	1.10.16	8.am	do.	

A W Barber A.R.E. Major R.E.
O.C. 124th Field Coy. R.E.

SECRET.

ORIGINAL WAR DIARY - NOVEMBER 1916.

124th. Field Company, Royal Engineers.
38th. (Welsh) Divn.

30th. November 1916.

Army Form C. 2118.

WAR DIARY
or
INTELLIGENCE SUMMARY.
(Erase heading not required.)

T.
14th Field Coy. Royal Engineers

Place	Date	Hour	Summary of Events and Information	Remarks and references to Appendices
Sheet N.W 28.0.3.3 C.19	1.11.16	11am	Left Sector – Ypres Salient. Work on Fargate Strong Point, Dugouts & New trenches. Patrolling and repairing bridges. Repairing Gympipe. Construction of Gym Boot Stores. Strong Signallers dug out. Billet dug outs etc in Ypres and Canal Banks continued. Constructing new trenches & dug outs in front line. Work on Snipers Post continued. No 1 Section in Rest Billets employed on works in back area. Major Kirkwood admitted to Hospital	
do	2.11.16		Ditto	
	3.11.16		Ditto	
	4.11.16		Ditto	
	5.11.16		Ditto	
	6.11.16		Ditto	
	7.11.16		Ditto	
	8.11.16		Ditto	
	9.11.16		Ditto	
	10.11.16		Ditto	
	11.11.16		Ditto	

WAR DIARY or INTELLIGENCE SUMMARY.

Army Form C. 2118.

179th Tunnel. Sp. Royal Engineers

Place	Date	Hour	Summary of Events and Information	Remarks and references to Appendices
Shg N.W C.19 C.3.3	12.11.16		Northern Sector – Ypres Salient. Work continued on Forgate Dugston Shrinky Points dug outs etc, also trucks and dug outs in front line. Repairing & extending tramways. Constructing new Bat stores & dug outs on Yprette and Canal Banks. Extending water trough in Yprette.	
	13.11.16		Ditto	
	14.11.16		Ditto	
	15.11.16		Ditto	
	16.11.16		Ditto. No 4 Section went to rest billet, No. 1 Section taking over work in Front Line	
	17.11.16		ditto	
	18.11.16		ditto	
	19.11.16		ditto	
	20.11.16		ditto	
	21.11.16		ditto	
	22.11.16		ditto 2/Lieut Powell admitted to Hospital	
	23.11.16		ditto	
	24.11.16		ditto	

WAR DIARY
INTELLIGENCE SUMMARY.

(Erase heading not required.) 11th Field Coy Royal Engineers

Army Form C. 2118.

Place	Date	Hour	Summary of Events and Information	Remarks and references to Appendices
Sheet NW.28 C.19.C.3.3	25.11.16		Northern Section Ypres Salient.	
	26.11.16		As for 12th.	
	27.11.16		Ditto	
	28.11.16		Ditto	
	29.11.16		Ditto	
	30.11.16		Ditto. No. 2 Section proceeds that Details, Work at Izenzule, Shipping etc. taken	
			over by No. 4 Section.	

R. Thacker
O.C. 11th Field Coy. R.E.

11 Lieut. R.E.

Vol 13

December 1916

Original War Diary.

124th Field Company R.E.
38th (Welsh) Division.

Army Form C. 2118.

127th Field Coy. Royal Engineers

WAR DIARY
or
INTELLIGENCE SUMMARY.
(Erase heading not required.)

Place	Date	Hour	Summary of Events and Information	Remarks and references to Appendices
Sheet NW36				
C19C3.3	1.12.16		Ypres Salient – Northern Sector. Work on Skipton & Argyle Strong Points &c. Repairing dugouts & trenches in front line. Extending & repairing tramways. Constructing dugouts etc. on Canal Bank. No. 2 Section in rest billets & employed on latter standings etc.	
	2.12.16		As for 1st	
	3.12.16		As for 1st. Capt. D. BAIRD R.E. resumed Command of Company. Lieut. Sellick admitted to Hospital.	
	4.12.16		Ditto.	
	5.12.16		Ditto.	
	6.12.16		Ditto.	
	7.12.16		Ditto.	
	8.12.16		Ditto.	
	9.12.16		Ditto.	
	10.12.16		Ditto.	
	11.12.16		Ditto.	
	12.12.16		Ditto. No.1 Section proceed to Reserve Billets. O.C. & Advance Party of 227 Field Coy RE arrived to take over work, stores, etc.	

Army Form C. 2118.

WAR DIARY
INTELLIGENCE SUMMARY.
(Erase heading not required.)

172th Field Coy. RE

Place	Date	Hour	Summary of Events and Information	Remarks and references to Appendices
C.19.c.3.3	13.12.16		Work handed over to 227 Field Coy. RE. Nos. 3 & 4 Sections proceeded to Not Lillers.	
Marckeghem	14.12.16		Company marched to Sarlock, and entrained there for Bollezeele, then marched to Merckeghem. Transport travelled by road.	
do	15.12.16		Improving billets. Inspections of kit and equipment.	
do	16.12.16		Training.	
do	17.12.16		do	
do	18.12.16		do	
do	19.12.16		Inspection of Company by Commander-in-Chief.	
do	20.12.16		Training.	
do	21.12.16		do	
do	22.12.16		do.	
do	23.12.16		Company proceeded to Watten.	
Watten	24.12.16		Training	
do	25.12.16		do	
do	26.12.16		do	
do	27.12.16		Pontooning and Route March.	

Army Form C. 2118.

WAR DIARY
or
INTELLIGENCE SUMMARY.

(Erase heading not required.)

(124th Field Coy. Royal Engineers)

Instructions regarding War Diaries and Intelligence Summaries are contained in F. S. Regs., Part II. and the Staff Manual respectively. Title pages will be prepared in manuscript.

Place	Date	Hour	Summary of Events and Information	Remarks and references to Appendices
WATTEN	28.12.16		Entraining and Route March	
do	29.12.16		do. OC proceeded to Elverdinghe to take over work from 123rd Field Coy. R.E.	
do	30.12.16		Company proceeded to Elverdinghe.	
Elverdinghe	31.12.16		Work Commenced in No.4 Left Sector, Ypres Salient.	

A.M. Barber Lieut. R.E.
for O.C. 124th Field Coy. R.E.

Secret. January 1917.

Original War Diary

Vol 14

124th Field Company R.E.
38th (Welsh) Division.

31-1-17.

Army Form C. 2118.

WAR DIARY
INTELLIGENCE SUMMARY.
(Erase heading not required.)

171st Field Coy. Royal Engineers

Place	Date	Hour	Summary of Events and Information	Remarks and references to Appendices
Elverdinghe	1.1.17.		Sheet 1 N.W. 28. Billet at A.18.b.1.8. Work on M.G. emplacements, Comm". trenches, Front Line, Support Line, Reserve Line, drainage, and erection of dugouts in new left sector (Boesinghe) Ypres Salient. Company working with 116th Infantry Brigade, 39th Division.	
do	2.1.17.		As for 1st.	
	3.1.17.		do 1st	
	4.1.17.		do 1st	
	5.1.17.		do 4th. No. 4 section proceeds to work on improving J.Camp.	
	6.1.17.		do 4th	
	7.1.17.		do 4th. 2/Lt J. Fowler from hospital 6.1.17.	
	8.1.17.		do 4th. Capt. A.S. Parker proceeds to leave to U.K. 7.1.17. 6.17.1.17.	
	9.1.17.		do 4th	
	10.1.17.		do 4th	
	11.1.17.		do 4th	
	12.1.17.		Coy. relieved by 151st Field Coy. R.E. and proceeds to H Camp at A.15.b.9.5.	
	13.1.17.		Coy. relieve 229th Field Coy. R.E. at C.19.c.2.3. Banks Brigade area Left Division Upper Salient. No. 1 section from J.Camp & No. 1 section to J.Camp.	

Army Form C. 2118.

WAR DIARY
INTELLIGENCE SUMMARY
(Erase heading not required.)

172st Field Coy. Royal Engineers

Instructions regarding War Diaries and Intelligence Summaries are contained in F. S. Regs., Part II. and the Staff Manual respectively. Title pages will be prepared in manuscript.

Sheet No. 28

Place	Date	Hour	Summary of Events and Information	Remarks and references to Appendices
Cq.C.23	14.1.17		Central Sector. Work on Front line E21+K D22, New Trench D22,t Kaling Comm trench. Sargate Strong Point. Extending repairing tramways. Constructing dug-outs etc on Canal Bank.	
	15.1.17	As for 14th		
	16.1.17	As for 14th		
	17.1.17	As for 14th		
	18.1.17	As for 14th	Capt Barber from leave.	
	19.1.17	As for 14th	Capt D'Baines to 2nd Army School	
	20.1.17	As for 19th	Capt Barber posted to 157 Coy R.E. Lt Ethersqan posted to Company from 157 Coy R.E. as A/Capt.	
	21.1.17	As for 20th		
	22.1.17	As for 20th		
	23.1.17	As for 20th		
	24.1.17	As for 20th		
	25.1.17	As for 20th		
	26.1.17	As for 20th		
	27.1.17	As for 20th		

Army Form C. 2118.

3.

121st Field Coy. R.E.

WAR DIARY
INTELLIGENCE SUMMARY.
(Erase heading not required.)

Instructions regarding War Diaries and Intelligence Summaries are contained in F. S. Regs., Part II. and the Staff Manual respectively. Title pages will be prepared in manuscript.

Place	Date	Hour	Summary of Events and Information	Remarks and references to Appendices
Sheet NW2 8.				
Cq. O23.	28.1.17	as pr 27th.		
	29.1.17	as pr 27th.		
	30.1.17	as pr 27th.		
	31.1.17	as pr 27th.		

Geo. Mapp
Capt. R.E.
O.C. 121st Field Coy. R.E.

2353 Wt. W2544/1454 700,000 5/15 D. D. & L. A.D.S.S./Forms/C. 2118.

"Secret"

Vol 15

Original War Diary February 1917.

124th Field Company. R.E.
38th (Welsh.) Division

Army Form C. 2118.

WAR DIARY
INTELLIGENCE SUMMARY.

1st K. Field Coy. R.E.

(Erase heading not required.)

Place	Date	Hour	Summary of Events and Information	Remarks and references to Appendices
Sheet 14 S 28	February			①
Coy C. 23.	1-2-17		Ypres Salient, Left Division, Central Sector: Strong point and extension. Erecting dug-outs on Canal Bank. Screening & repairing bridges. Repairing and extending tramways. Constructing new trenches and dug-outs in front lines. No.1 Section employed on works at J. Camp.	
	2-2-17		A.1 for 1st Capt. D. Paird from G.H.Q. 2-2-17	
	3-2-17		Ad for 2nd	
	4-2-17		do	
	5-2-17		do	
	6-2-17		do	
	7-2-17		do	
	8-2-17		do	
	9-2-17		do	
	10-2-17		do	
	11-2-17		do	
	12-2-17		do	

Army Form C. 2118.

WAR DIARY
or
INTELLIGENCE SUMMARY.

174th. Field Coy. R.E.

(Erase heading not required.)

Instructions regarding War Diaries and Intelligence Summaries are contained in F.S. Regs., Part II. and the Staff Manual respectively. Title pages will be prepared in manuscript.

Place	Date	Hour	Summary of Events and Information	Remarks and references to Appendices
Ouest N.W.28				
Sq.C.2.3.	13.2.17		Central Sector. Left Division Ypres Salient. Report 12th. 1 Sapper slightly wounded.	
	14.2.17		Report 13th.	
	15.2.17		Report 13th. one Sapper accidently wounded (Miguel) by a rifle being accidentally	
	16.2.17		Report 13th. (fired in a dug-out.	
	17.2.17		Report 13th.	
	18.2.17		Report 13th. 2 NCO's & 7 Sappers took part in a raid on an enemy's trenches with 14th. R.I.R. military at about 1am 18/7/17. Each carried a pickel, ten fuzes with ammonal, to wreck emplacements etc. No emplacements have found + explosives were fired in enemy's front line. 1NCO & 2 Sappers wounded.	
	19.2.17		Report 18th. 2nd Lt. G. Begg appointed Assistant Field Engineer to CE. XIV Corps.	
	20.2.17		do	
	21.2.17		do	
	22.2.17		do Court of Enquiry held to investigate the circumstances under which 144512 Sapper G. Berry was accidentally wounded. 15/2/17	
	23.2.17		Report 22nd. (i) Lt. P.G. Daniels joined Coy from No.4. F.B.D.	

WAR DIARY
INTELLIGENCE SUMMARY.

(Erase heading not required.) 172nd Field Coy. R.E.

Army Form C. 2118.

Place	Date	Hour	Summary of Events and Information	Remarks and references to Appendices
A9C7.2.	24.2.17	As for 23rd	One sapper slightly wounded.	
	25.2.17	As for 24th		
	26.2.17	do.		
	27.2.17	do.		
	28.2.17	do.		

J. Stewart
Capt. R.E.
O.C. 172nd Field Coy. R.E.

Secret.

No 16

Original War Diary - March 1917.

124th Field Company Royal Engineers
38th (Welsh) Division

31. 3. 17.

Army Form C. 2118.

12th Field Company R.E.

WAR DIARY
or
INTELLIGENCE SUMMARY.

(Erase heading not required.)

Place	Date	Hour	Summary of Events and Information	Remarks and references to Appendices
Sheet 28 NW				
C19.C.2.3.1-3-17			Ypres Salient. Lancashire Sector (Left Division) Work continued on targets. Coy: I Sunk entered to forward saps and track Communication to front line. Sucking Company Headquarters in support lines and Posts, with 5.9 shell proof Elephant Shelto dugouts. Reclaiming front line and constructing new fire trench. Sucking 5.9 shellproof dugouts along W.side of Canal Bank and making existing dugouts 5.9 shell proof. Continued work on Tramway repairs and extensions, and general maintenance of Bridges. No3 Section employed on New Devonshire & J Camp.	
"	2-3-17		As for 1st	
"	3-3-17		do.	
"	4-3-17		do.	
"	5-3-17		do.	
"	6-3-17		do.	
"	7-3-17		do.	
"	8-3-17		do.	

WAR DIARY
or
INTELLIGENCE SUMMARY

Army Form C. 2118.

2 124 Field Company R.E.

Place	Date	Hour	Summary of Events and Information	Remarks and references to Appendices
Shed 28				
C.19.c.23.	9.3.17	9.30am	do for 8th	
	10.3.17		do One Sapper wounded in Lunch Tramway.	
	11-3-17		do	
	12-3-17		do	
	13-3-17		do	
	14-3-17		do	
	15-3-17		Enemy shelled with 5.9 shells the area in front of Dugouts occupied by the Company. Casualties 3 Sappers killed and 1 wounded.	
	16-3-17		do for 14th	
	17-3-17		Enemy raided that line trenches, under cover of a heavy artillery bombardment, in two parties, one each side of a small working party of R.E.s and attached infantry. Casualties:- 1 Sapper and 2 attached Infantry missing, and one attached Infantry wounded.	
	18-3-17		do for 16th	
	19-3-17		do	
	20-3-17		do	

Army Form C. 2118.

124 Field Company, R.E.

WAR DIARY
or
INTELLIGENCE SUMMARY.

(Erase heading not required.)

Instructions regarding War Diaries and Intelligence Summaries are contained in F. S. Regs., Part II. and the Staff Manual respectively. Title pages will be prepared in manuscript.

Place	Date	Hour	Summary of Events and Information	Remarks and references to Appendices
Shed 28 N.W.				
C.19.C.2.3.	21-3-17		as for the 20th	
	22-3-17		do	
	23-3-17		do	
	24-3-17		do	
	25-3-17		do	
	26-3-17		do	
	27-3-17		do	
	28-3-17		do	
	29-3-17		do	
	30-3-17		do	
	30-3-17		do.	

Capt. R.E.
O.C. 124 Field Company R.E.

Secret

Original War Diary - April 1917.

124th Field Coy Royal Engineers
38th (Welsh) Division

30/4/17.

WAR DIARY or INTELLIGENCE SUMMARY

Army Form C. 2118.

Ry. Field Coy R.E. I

Place	Date	Hour	Summary of Events and Information	Remarks and references to Appendices
Shw 28 NW. C.19.c.2.3.	1-4-17		Ypres Salient Left Division (Centre Section) Continued work on Target Coy = trees to forward stops. "Comm'l trench" from Target to Front line known as Bain trench. Reclaiming that line by cutting a new track behind parapet & revetting (wire & two cwts.) front line trenchwork. From Zwietee main trenchwork. New Coy HQ for Infantry in front line being erected to stand 5.9 enemy crl. fire one section employed on west bank of Yser Canal making existing dugouts for Reserve Batt's 5.9 shell proof and maintaining tramway line from Rt Dumps to front line. Mules employed (in stabling the tram along the tramway also for tanking excavation and removing earth from west of Ypres to the top of Dugouts on west bank of Yser Canal. All Company Transport fully employed. Divisioner, CRE and Company work. hauling timber, RE material Etc. Plans drawn up for Camouflage RE Dumps, Australia and Belmont, on Ypres-Boesinghe Railway line, and passed on to CRE for approval.	
	2-4-17		Continued work as above.	

WAR DIARY
or
INTELLIGENCE SUMMARY. 124 7th Coy RE

(Erase heading not required.)

Army Form C. 2118.

Place	Date	Hour	Summary of Events and Information	Remarks and references to Appendices
Shd 2PN/W.				
C.19,C.2.8.	3-4-17		Continued work as for 2nd. Plans for camouflage of Dumps passed by CRE and work commenced on Austerity Dump.	
	4-4-17		Continued work as for 3rd.	
	5-4-17		do.	
	6-4-17		do.	
	7-4-17		do.	
	8-4-17		do.	
	9-4-17		do. Capt C.V. Morgan RE proceeded to Paris on duty for CRE.	
	10-4-17		do.	
	11-4-17		do.	
	12-4-17		do.	
	13-4-17		do.	
	14-4-17		do.	
	15-4-17		do.	
	16-4-17		do.	
	17-4-17		Regtl Brigade area split up, the right half taken over by the 39th Div.	

WAR DIARY
or
INTELLIGENCE SUMMARY

124 H.Coy R.E. III

Army Form C. 2118.

Place	Date	Hour	Summary of Events and Information	Remarks and references to Appendices
Sheet 28 N.W.				
C19.C.2.3.	18-4-17		and the Entire Section taken over by the right Bayonet, and the area to be known as the Lancashire Farm Section. R.E. went in with out-section of old night Bayonet handed over to the 123rd Field Co. R.E., also Australian R.E Dump and Tramway from same to front line, also all went on 10 dugouts on East Bank of Yser Canal.	
	19-4-17		Continued work as before in left area, No 4 Section previously employed in right area, commenced work on acting a new tram line below existing (party away) tractivers from Harbour turnout tramway to Baird Trench. Capt G.V.Maggard returned from duty at Paris.	
	20-4-17		Continued work as above. Camouflage work at Retmol Dump carried on and tramway trees laid down for having tramtram during the day.	
	21-4-17		do.	
	22-4-17		do.	

WAR DIARY
INTELLIGENCE SUMMARY

Army Form C. 2118.

124 Field Coy RE IV

Place	Date	Hour	Summary of Events and Information	Remarks and references to Appendices
Shw 28 N.W. C.19.a.3.2.	23-4-17		Ypres Salient. Left Division's right Brigade. Kemmelin Farm Sector. Continued work as for 22nd	
	24-4-17		do. Commenced loading RE material at Belmont Dump during daylight. No 82333 Sapr Wood of this Coy. wounded when in charge of a large infantry party employed reclaiming trench for fire trench, the party were caught in a heavy bombardment, and suffered casualties, 3 killed, 8 wounded and 3 shell wounds.	
	25-4-17		Continued work as for 24.17.	
	26-4-17		do. 14 Sappers attached to join the 13th West Rgt. for Demolition work.	
	27-4-17		do.	
	28-4-17		do.	
	29-4-17		do. The 14 Sappers attached Batt. Raiding party were inspected by the Corps Commander.	
	30-4-17		do. Heavy artillery bombardment during the night on Enemy Lines. Enquiries successfully raised.	

Geo. Morgan Capt 124th RE
to O.C. 124 Coy

Secret.

Original War Diary - May. 1917.

124th Field Company R.E.
38th Welsh Division

31.5.1917

WAR DIARY
INTELLIGENCE SUMMARY. 2nd N. Coy R.E.

Army Form C. 2118.

Place	Date	Hour	Summary of Events and Information	Remarks and references to Appendices
Sheet 28 N.W. C.19.c.3.2.	1st May 1917		**Ypres Salient Left Division Right Brigade.** The 13th West Regiment carried out a very successful raid on the enemy trenches on a front of several hundred yards. One NCO and thirteen sappers from this Company were attached to the raiding party for blowing up dugouts and M.G. Emplacements. Twelve prisoners are captured and one Trench Mortar. The Sapper party entered the enemy trenches with the Infantry and did very good work. 5 Concrete Dugouts, 1 Concrete M.G. Emplacement, and 3 Heavy Trench Mortars were blown up. L/Cpl Jones No 1100 (No 62885) in charge of the Sapper party and Sapper J.H. Davies (No 62620), S.W. Evrad (No 63692) and P. Frampton (No 62623) did very excellent work, and returned again to "No Mans Land" to carry on the work under heavy fire. No 1 section employed burying Concrete Dugouts in Tangate String Point, also reclaiming the communication trench (Upper Tangate) towards the extreme left post in front near Yn Canal Bank.	

Army Form C. 2118.

WAR DIARY
INTELLIGENCE SUMMARY
(Erase heading not required.)

1/1 Field Coy. N.Z.

Place	Date	Hour	Summary of Events and Information	Remarks and references to Appendices
Sheet 28 N.W. C.19.C.2.3.	1 May 1917		Also continued work making Company H.Q. Dugouts in the Sunken Dugouts in West Canal Bank of Yser Canal 5'.9" shell proof. No. 3 Section employed making wiring 5'.9" shell proof, also maintenance of Tramways, and the building of a new Brigade Headquarters. No. 4 Section employed reclaiming or parts and cutting a new front line trench from Bavaria trench northwards and southwards to Hackwood trench. Etc. No. 2 Section employed as Divisional School mover Divisional Headquarters.	
	2nd May 1917		do. for 1st	
	3rd "		do	
	4th "		do	
	5th "		do	
	6th "		do	
	7th "		do	
	8th "		work on until 7th. No. 92575 Sapper D.M. Grace of this Company	

Army Form C. 2118.

WAR DIARY
INTELLIGENCE SUMMARY.

(Erase heading not required.)

2nd & 1st Coy. R.E.

Instructions regarding War Diaries and Intelligence Summaries are contained in F. S. Regs., Part II. and the Staff Manual respectively. Title pages will be prepared in manuscript.

Place	Date	Hour	Summary of Events and Information	Remarks and references to Appendices
Shw 28 N.W. C.19, C.2,3.	8th May 1917		Lines by Field General Court martial at Company Headquarters C.19, C.2,3. sent as for 8th	
	9th		Funeral & Tullas General Court martial on Sapper Grace promulgated and sentenced to 90 days F.P. N°.1.	
	10th		Work as for the 9th.	
	11th		Work as for the 10th. also repairing and making gun wells, turner in the old farms near the Front Line. Sappers Line Boothe on fire.	
	12th		As for Coys. for Julius Wells suppliers.	
	13th		As for the 11th.	
	14th		Work as for the 13th. The Enemy attempted to raid the Front line trenches in the right sub-sector (Lancashire Farm sector) at 3 am under cover of a heavy Artillery bombardment. The raid was successfully repulsed by our infantry. The raiding party which was believed to be about 40 strong retired leaving behind the bodies of the raid who was wounded, and eventually brought in and now prisoner. Heavy casualties are believed to have been inflicted on the raiders.	

2353 Wt. W2544/1454 700,000 5/15 D.D. & L. A.D.S.S./Forms/C. 2118.

Army Form C. 2113.

WAR DIARY
INTELLIGENCE SUMMARY
(Erase heading not required.)

124th Z. In Col. R.E.

Instructions regarding War Diaries and Intelligence Summaries are contained in F. S. Regs., Part II. and the Staff Manual respectively. Title pages will be prepared in manuscript.

Place	Date	Hour	Summary of Events and Information	Remarks and references to Appendices
Shl 28 N10				
C.19.c.2.3.	15 May 1917		Worked for the 14th. No 2 Section returned from Divisional School.	
	16th		do. No 62831 T/Cpl. C.W. Jose and No 62692 Sapper S.W. Grist of this Company awarded the Military Medal for meritorious act performed on the night of 30th April/1st May 1917 during a raid on the enemy trenches. 2nd Lieut. E.O. Dunn R.E. returned from leave to England.	
	17th		Worked as for 16th.	
	18th		do for 17th	
	19th		" " "	
	20th		" " "	
	21st		" " "	
	22nd		" " "	
	23rd		" " "	
	24th		Worked for 392nd Tramways Landed over Lt. Tramway Co. R.E.	
	25th		do for 24th Company Officer making Reconnaisance in "No mans land" for offensive operations.	
	26th		Worked as for 25th. Continue preparation for offensive operations.	

WAR DIARY

INTELLIGENCE SUMMARY.

Ref. F. ½ Coy. R.E.

Army Form C. 2118.

Place	Date	Hour	Summary of Events and Information	Remarks and references to Appendices
Sheet 28 N.W.				
C.19, C.2.3.	27th May 1917		Work as for 26th.	
	28th "		Reconnaissance made of "Hanna Lane" and new front line and five communication trenches marked out with Spurgam.	
	29th "		all work stopped	
	30th "		night of 29th-30th The whole Company employed digging communication trenches to new front line. Three Batts of Infantry employed digging new front line trench from near Canea rose northwards to Canal Bank. Work completed (and wire entanglement) by 2-30 a.m. Casualties 1- RE and attached Infantry. Infantry 3 killed 14 wounded.	
	31st "		Batts digging front line and evening, RE and attached Infantry employed in support digging extra communication trench to new front line. Work completed satisfactory.	

Geo Morgan
Capt RE
O.C. 1/2 Field Coy
RE.

Secret

Original War Diary June 1917.

124th Field Company Royal Engineers
38th (Welsh) Division

30-6-17

WAR DIARY

Army Form C. 2118.

I. 124 Field Co. Royal Engineers

Place	Date	Hour	Summary of Events and Information	Remarks and references to Appendices
Sheet 28 NW				
C.19.0.2.B.	1st June 1917		Ypres Salient. Left Division, Right Brigade (Lancashire Fusm. Bde.in) No.1 section employed reclaiming old Seaforth trench from Canal Bank eastwards to old hot line. Dismd. through Canal Bank from Targa6 entrance camp Also. Continued work making new Company Headquarters Dugouts at western slope 5'9 dead point. No 2 Section reclaiming old front line from Baird Communication Trench northwards to join up with the new lines at old Seaforth. Deepening and revetting Communication trench No 9 and pushing forward, from extreme north point of new front line trench on East side of Ypres Canal, in a S.E. direction eventually join up with new Comn Trench No. 9. (in no mans land). No 3 section employed on Canal Bank (west side) making new Elephant Shed Shelters, extending old area + 24ft long, and making roofs of same 5'9 dead point. Supervision and repair of Bridges. No 3 Section making new Communication Trench from Canal Bank easterly Boundry Trench to Colne Valley. Coy.	
	2nd June 1917		Work as for the 1st. Company Dugouts new heavies shells at 2 AM.	

Army Form C. 2118.

WAR DIARY
or
~~INTELLIGENCE SUMMARY.~~
(Erase heading not required.)

124 Field Co. R.E.

Place	Date	Hour	Summary of Events and Information	Remarks and references to Appendices
Ches 28/N.W.			(Continued)	
C.19.c.2.3.	2nd Jan 1917		One a direct hit obtained on Officers Latrine & Officers Cookhouse, also two direct hits on dugouts, but very little damage done, no casualties.	
	3rd "	"	Work as for 2nd. Previous artillery bombardment during the day.	
	"	"	Enemy bombarded back area with Gas and Incendiary shells, see narrative at "Stand to" from 11 pm to 1.30 AM.	
	4th "	"	Work as for the 3rd.	
	5th "	"	Work as for 3rd.	
	6th "	"	do	
	7th "	"	do	
	8th "	"	do	
	9th "	"	no.	
	10th "	"	do	
	11th "	"	do. One Sapper Killed, one Sapper & one attached Infantry wounded. Capt. Baird granted leave to Paris for seven days.	
	12th "	"	Work as for 11th. Area in vicinity of Company dug-outs bombarded, direct hit obtained on Officers Cookhouse.	

WAR DIARY

Army Form C. 2118.

III

12th Field Coy. R.E.

Instructions regarding War Diaries and Intelligence Summaries are contained in F. S. Regs., Part II. and the Staff Manual respectively. Title pages will be prepared in manuscript.

(Erase heading not required.)

Place	Date	Hour	Summary of Events and Information	Remarks and references to Appendices
Sheet 28. N.W. C.19.C.2.3			(Continued)	
	12th June 1917		Gas shells also dropped. Respirators worn for half hour.	
	13th	"	Work as for 12th up to midday. Company relieved by 123rd Army Coy R.E.	
			Company proceeded to transport lines at G. Camp.	
			Relief complete by 6 p.m.	
	14th	"	Company moved from G. Camp to Watten for training, demonstrated by French transport by road via Leggare Cappel. Company arrived Watten 2.30 p.m.	
	15th	"	Transport arrived 10.30 p.m. Company attaches infantry. Commenced training, still musketry, bayonet fighting, pontooning etc.	
	16th	"	Training gas for 15th. Various training for offensive operations.	
	17th	"	do	
	18th	"	do. Capt. D. Baird from Paris.	
	19th	"	do	
	20th	"	do	
	21st	"	do	
	22nd	"	do	

Army Form C. 2118.

WAR DIARY
or
INTELLIGENCE SUMMARY.

(Erase heading not required.)

IV / 124th Field Coy. R.E.

Instructions regarding War Diaries and Intelligence Summaries are contained in F.S. Regs., Part II. and the Staff Manual respectively. Title pages will be prepared in manuscript.

Place	Date	Hour	Summary of Events and Information	Remarks and references to Appendices
Watten	23.6.17		Company marched from Watten to Argues. Bivouac the night in Argues.	
	24.6.17		Company marched from Argues to Romely.	
	25.6.17		Officers & Senior N.C.O. proceed to training area and commence laying out a replica of the trenches for Offensive operations. Remainder of Company & attached Infantry Drilling, Musketry etc.	
	26.6.17		O.C. & 2/Lt _____ attached Infantry proceed to Training Ground, Work R.	
	27.6.17		Company move from Romely to Boncourt.	
	28.6.17		O.C. & 2/Lt _____ Officers N.C.O. & attached Infantry continue work on Training Ground.	
	29.6.17 30.6.17		Work as 28th. Whole Coy. and attached Infantry work on Training area. do.	

Geo. Ynorgan Capt RE
for Major RE
O.C. 124th Field Coy RE.

Secret.   July. 1917.

Original War Diary.

124th Field Company. R.E.

38th (Welsh) Division

21. 8. 17.

WAR DIARY
or
INTELLIGENCE SUMMARY.
(Erase heading not required.)

Army Form C. 2118.

I to field Coy R.E.

124 - Field Coy. R.E.

Place	Date	Hour	Summary of Events and Information	Remarks and references to Appendices
St Riquier Hay Block Sq.	Doncourt 1-7-17		Company and attached employed at laying out a replica of the trenches for offensive action. Musketry etc.	
	2.7.17		do. Gunnery drill.	
	3.7.17		do. Capt. G.W.Morgan to CR.E. to take spell at adj. 2/Lt.A.Brazel fires Corp.	
	4.7.17		do.	
	5.7.17		do. 2/Lt.G.M. here at H.Q. picture of 1097. Pte Taylor 15 R.W.F. attached.	
	6.7.17		do. Making target etc.	
	7.7.17		do. do.	
	8.7.17		Took us for 9th. Pte. Taylor sentence promulgated 2 years S.H.	
	9.7.17		do.	
	10.7.17		do.	
	11.7.17		do.	
	12.7.17		Divisional conf. on taining ground.	
	13.7.17		Taining drill etc.	
	14.7.17		" Company Sports & Concert.	

WAR DIARY

Army Form C. 2118.

II 1/4th Field Coy RE

Place	Date	Hour	Summary of Events and Information	Remarks and references to Appendices
Hazebrouck Sta	15.7.17		Packing of Company transport ready to move.	
Boncourt	16.7.17		Company entrained Infantry move at 6-30am. 16 January arriving at 3pm.	
	17.7.17		Company near to Caëstre area.	
	18.7.17		Company move to Becke.	
	19.7.17		Company move from Becke to Proven area.	
	20.7.17		Night of 20/21st relieved 49th Field Coy RE (Kents) in Jumnah of sectr	
			XIV Corps Area 1 killed + 16 wounded on march, near Elverdinghe.	
	21.7.17		Work on Marengo Causeway. Glympse Cottage Iran Line Bridges Brigade H.Q. T.M. E.S.L. Targets etc. 1 Man wounded night of 21/22nd	
	22.7.17		Work as 21st. Gas shell bombardment night of 21/22nd. Box respirators worn for 5½ hours. 1 hope wounded.	
	23.7.17		Work as for 22nd. Majority of Company sick from Gas poisoning (previous nght).	
	24.7.17		do Gas shell bombardment (night of 23/24) 21 Sappers to hospital.	
	Do		Major Stark + Lt E. Shee to hospital.	

WAR DIARY
or
~~INTELLIGENCE SUMMARY.~~
(Erase heading not required.)

Army Form C. 2118.

III
12th Field Coy. R.E.

Place	Date	Hour	Summary of Events and Information	Remarks and references to Appendices
Sh.27 NW				
B.24 & 92	25/7/17 26/7/17 27/7/17		Zonnebeke Ypres Salient. Took as for 24th. Work as for 28th. Company now north of Ylvs. S.-b. no. Wire received 1/30p. Staib 6. Advance commenced in bounds at 5/15 am.	
	28/7/17		Work on Mauringe barracual. No further advance. Company standing by. No supps dept arrived. 1 Supp. 2 atts Mg. tommes.	
	29/7/17 30/7/17		Work as 28th. 2 Supps 2 atts Mg. tommies. do Company now 6 dug outs south of Bridge 5.	
			Orders received from C.R.E. for work on Z day. "12th Fd. Coy. R.E. will proceed made strong points lot. 1-8. (See attd sketch) on receipt of information that fights to firmly established in 'BLACK LINE'." (Zero 3-50 am. 31-7-17)	
	31/7/17		Company standing b[y] at 4.45 am. Officers sent to 113 + 114 Brigade H.Q. to keep in touch with progress of advance. 7.20am. information received from 113 Brigades fighting firmly established in Black Line. 7.30am Company.	

WAR DIARY or INTELLIGENCE SUMMARY

Army Form C. 2118.

N° 124 F.A. Coy. R.E.

Place	Date	Hour	Summary of Events and Information	Remarks and references to Appendices
	31/7/17 Continued		Left Canal Bank to construct Strong Points 1-8. Took first concentrated on Points 1-4, which were placed in state of defence by midday. (Was attached to Section left at 11:30am.) Sections left to complete S.P.s 1-4 & to construct Strong Points 5-8. Took had been commenced by garrisons (except at No. 8) when Sections arrived. Work of wiring & improving S.P.s was proceeded with and Strong Points put in a state of defence by 6:30-7pm. S.P.s no. 4 & 8 were shelled throughout the day, as also were 2, 3 & 7 during the afternoon. Casualties R.E. 2 killed, 12 wounded, 4 missing believed killed. Attached Infy. 1 killed, 7 wounded, 2 missing believed killed.	

R. Bright
O.C. 124 F.A. Coy. R.E.

Secret.

Vol 2

Original War Diary - August 1917.

124th Field Coy. Royal Engineers
38th (Welsh) Division.

Army Form C. 2118.

WAR DIARY
or
INTELLIGENCE SUMMARY.
(Erase heading not required.)

12st. 4th y Cy. R.E.

Place	Date	Hour	Summary of Events and Information	Remarks and references to Appendices
Shot 28 MM	August 1917			
C.29.c.25.	1st.	10 am.	Zonnebek Sect. Ypres Salient. Took on Strong Point No. 1 to 8, completing wiring & draining.	
	2.		Looking on Gypsum Cottage tramway, covering tramps pickets & repairing working line.	
	3rd		Work as for 2nd.	
	4th		Work as for 2nd.	
	5th		The Sapper Sormany. Company relieved by 84th Field Coy R.E. 26th Division. Proceeds to Wieltje Camp.	
	6th		Company resting whole day.	
	7th		Overhauling & fitting 6 Ford Cars & Company tools, cleaning vehicles etc.	
	8.		Work as for 7th.	
	9th		Company move to camp at E.4.C.6.1. to work on Swimming Baths at E.3.a.q.3.	
	10th		Work on Swimming Baths. Pumping water from excavation.	
	11th		Work on Baths.	

Army Form C. 2118.

WAR DIARY
or
INTELLIGENCE SUMMARY.   124 F. Coy. R.E.
(Erase heading not required.)

Instructions regarding War Diaries and Intelligence Summaries are contained in F. S. Regs., Part II. and the Staff Manual respectively. Title pages will be prepared in manuscript.

Place	Date	Hour	Summary of Events and Information	Remarks and references to Appendices
Stewy.				
E.u.E.S.I	12th		Work on Baths.	
	13th		do.	
	14th		do.	
	15th		do.	
	16th		do.	
	17th		Concreting Commenced.	
			Work on Baths until 12/noon. Divisional Pioneers move to (3pm). Bivouacs at B.21.d.57. (by train from Steenwerck to Elverdinghe.)	pg n 4
			Work reconnoitred by O.C. Prior to relieving 85th Fld Coy R.E.	
	18th		Transport move from Steenwerck Camp at Steenvorde arrived B.21.a.57.	
		10 am.	Company moved to Coney Park, at ≡ Steenw.	
			H.Q. billet at C.19.c.3.3. Work commenced on Tramway.	
			Lieut A.N. Souter joined Company from Base.	
			acting Captain leave to England.	
	19th		Work on Tramways from Bridge 6.6. Steenvoorde Town and	
			continuation to 19 B.	
	20th		Monday to 19 B.	

WAR DIARY

INTELLIGENCE SUMMARY. 124th Fd. Coy. R.E. III

Army Form C. 2118.

Place	Date	Hour	Summary of Events and Information	Remarks and references to Appendices
C.19.C.33.	21st		Work on Tramway.	
	22nd		do	
	23rd		do	
	24th		do. Tramway through to the INGS. Company	
	25th		Move to billets on Canal Bank at Bn. H.Q.	
			Work on Tramway. & light infantry bridge line across the	
			Steenbeek for operation on 27th. 2 att. pkts missing.	
	26th		Tramway	
	27th		do. Bridges for tramway over Steenbeek complete.	
	28th		do. Lt. Gunn to Hospital	
	29th		do	
	30th		do	
	31st		do	

W Brush Capt R.E.
O.C. 124th Fd. Coy. R.E.

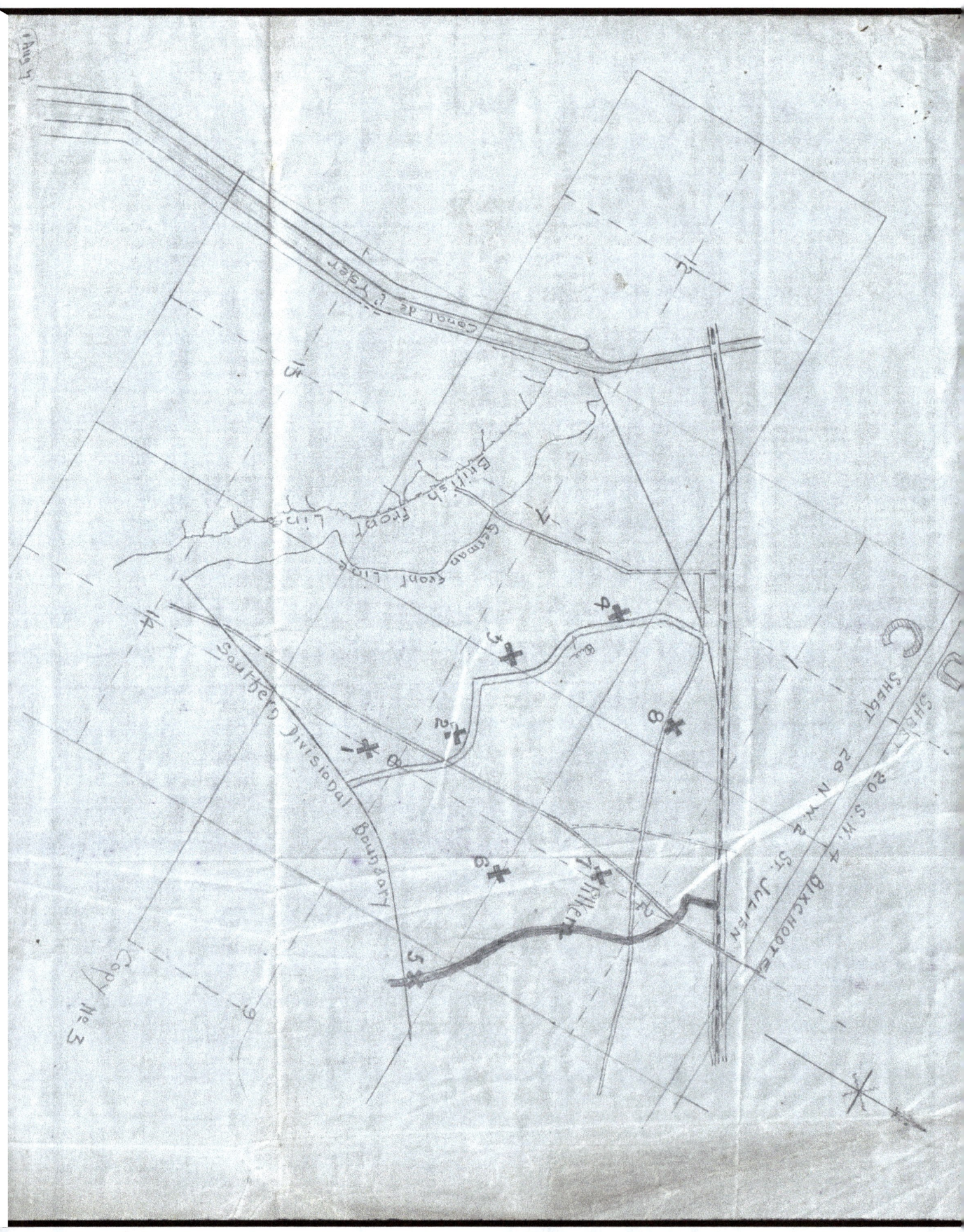

ANNEXE TO 124TH FIELD COY. R.E. WAR DIARY FOR AUGUST 1917.

PROGRESS OF WORK ON TRAMWAYS.

Date.	Yards of track laid.	Yards Sleepered.	Yards Duckboarded.	
21st August 1917.	400	300	100	
22nd do do	210	360	120	
23rd do do	270	320	155	
24th do do	480	350	—	
25th do do	240	310	60	
26th do do	345	220	140	
27th do do	80	160		Work impeded owing to heavy shell fire
28th do do	—	—	—	
28th do do	175	150	120	
29th do do	210	40	190	
30th do do	80	290	180	Work impeded owing to heavy shell fire.
	2490	2500	1065	

Capt. R.E.
O.C. 124th Field Coy. R.E.

Army Form C. 2118.

WAR DIARY
or
INTELLIGENCE SUMMARY.   124 Fd. Coy. R.E.

(Erase heading not required.)

Instructions regarding War Diaries and Intelligence Summaries are contained in F. S. Regs., Part II. and the Staff Manual respectively. Title pages will be prepared in manuscript.

Place	Date	Hour	Summary of Events and Information	Remarks and references to Appendices
Spot 28 M.M.	1917			
Bzd 6.9.6.	Sept 1.		Surprise attack. Free situation. Company billets on Lavac Brie. R.	
	2.		Road appr. 15. one Sapr. Wounds. Lt. Col. R.S. Philpots CRE took on damage to Abeele farm.	
	3.		Roads on tramways to Abeele farm.	
	4.		Works on tramways. One Sapr. Wounded.	
	5.		do. One Sapr. Wounded.	
	6.		do. Capt Boultis (?) gas to hospital. 627 676 927	
	7.		do. One Sapr. Wounded.	
	8.		do. One Sapr. Wounded.	
	9.		do.	
	10.		Company relieved by 83rd Fd. Coy. R.E. 20th Division. move to Gretve Farm.	
	11.		Company move to Brandhoek Reception Area. In Brampton Hospital.	
	12.		do	
	13.		Move to EECKE. Billet at Q.19.a & T.1. Sect. 3.	

WAR DIARY
or
INTELLIGENCE SUMMARY. 124 Fd. Cy. R.E.

Army Form C. 2118.

II

(Erase heading not required.)

Place	Date	Hour	Summary of Events and Information	Remarks and references to Appendices
Sheet 36 N.W.				
Q.M.Aug:	13th		Company moved to Mohegan Area	
	15th		Marched in Penrhiw Area	
	16th		Company moved to Kemmain	
			124 Fd. Cy. R.E. 51st Division Relieves 421st (West Lancashire)	
			Field Cy. R.E. in Farm at H.15.d.0.0. Sh: L.28 N.W.	
	19th		Officers N.C.Os reconnoitred work.	
			Company took on two from am; began any. V.C. O.R.	
			Kw. a. Bois Noirs Supply K.P.S for the Engineers	
			Moeves D.T.M. etc. Also property on drainage.	
	19th	do	Work as to 15th.	
	20th	" do		
	21st	do		
	22nd	do		
	23rd	do		
	24th	do		
	25th	do		
	26th	do	2 Lt. Jacob granted leave to U.K. from 26.9.17 to 6.10.17	

Army Form C. 2118.

WAR DIARY
or
INTELLIGENCE SUMMARY.
(Erase heading not required.)

124 Fd Coy R.E. III

Instructions regarding War Diaries and Intelligence Summaries are contained in F.S. Regs., Part II. and the Staff Manual respectively. Title pages will be prepared in manuscript.

Place	Date	Hour	Summary of Events and Information	Remarks and references to Appendices
Sheet 36 NW				
H.15.d.0.1.	27th		Work on fr. 26. No.1 Section on back area roads under C.R.E.	
	28th		do	
	29th		do	
	30th		do	

C.N.Brazel
Major R.E.
O.C. 124 Fd Coy R.E.

WAR DIARY
or
~~INTELLIGENCE~~ SUMMARY.
(Erase heading not required.)

Army Form C. 2118.

12th Fd. Coy. R.E. Vol 2

Place	Date	Hour	Summary of Events and Information	Remarks and references to Appendices
Sheet 36NW F.15.A.0.1.	Oct 1917 1st		Newhaven Sect. Work as for Sept. C.T.S. Drainage	
			O.Ps. M.G.S. T.M.Es	
	2nd		Work as for 1st	
	3rd		do	
	4th		do	
	5th		do	
	6th		do	
			2/Lt W.J. Watts to hospital	
	7th		do	
	8th		2/Lt Smith from leave 7-10-17. Work as for 6th	
			Work as for 7th	
	9th		do. Major C.H. Bagot granted leave to U.K. from 9.10.17 to 23.10.17	
	10th		do	
	11th		do. 2 Sappers wounded at V.C.O.P.	
	12th		do	
	13th		do	
	14th		do. 2/Lt H.C. Quine joined Coy from France 14/10/17	
	15th		do.	

Army Form C. 2118.

WAR DIARY
or
INTELLIGENCE SUMMARY.
(Erase heading not required.)

Instructions regarding War Diaries and Intelligence Summaries are contained in F. S. Regs., Part II. and the Staff Manual respectively. Title pages will be prepared in manuscript.

124th Ft. Coy. R.E.

Place	Date	Hour	Summary of Events and Information	Remarks and references to Appendices
Shut Johns	Oct 17			
Ardol.	16th		Work asp 15th.	
	17th		do.	
	18th		do.	
	19th		do.	
	20th		do.	
	21st		1 Sapp. killed 1 wounded by aeroplane bomb.	
	22nd		do.	
	23rd		do.	
	24th		do.	
	25th		Attached Infantry transferred 65 from 123rd Ft. Coy. R.E.	
	26th		do.	
	27th		do. Arrived Major C.H. Brazel from leave.	
	28th		Work asp 27th.	
	29th		do.	
	30th		do.	
	31st		do.	

C.H. Brazel
Major R.E.
O.C. 124 Ft. Coy. R.E.

WAR DIARY
or
INTELLIGENCE SUMMARY.   124th Field Coy. R.E.

Army Form C. 2118.

Place	Date	Hour	Summary of Events and Information	Remarks and references to Appendices
Nov 30 N.M.3				
A.15.a.1.0	1-11-17	10 a.m.	Newbridock. Left Division XI Corps. Company went to Corps	
			Reserve. Relieving Tin Barn Avenue, Cellar Farm Avenue,	
			Devon Avenue, Gurneys Avenue. Strength + Prisoners	
			over Canal. St Yves grates bar 6 N.R. from 1-11-17 6 to 15/11/17	
	2.11.17		as normal	
	3.11.17		do Company increased	
	4.11.17		Sunday - Day off - Coy. Football Team played St Yves + drew	
			1 core. 3-6-3.	
	5.11.17			
	6.11.17			
	7.11.17			
	8.11.17			
	9.11.17			
	10.11.17			
	11.11.17		Sunday - Day off - Football Team played 1st Welsh Scottish + won	
			1 core. 10 goals 6 nil.	

Army Form C. 2118.

WAR DIARY
or
INTELLIGENCE SUMMARY.

124th Field Coy. R.E.

(Erase heading not required.)

Instructions regarding War Diaries and Intelligence Summaries are contained in F.S. Regs., Part II. and the Staff Manual respectively. Title pages will be prepared in manuscript.

Place	Date	Hour	Summary of Events and Information	Remarks and references to Appendices
H.d.10	12.11.17	noon	Ao Fr. 10 F.	
	13.11.17			
	14.11.17			
	15.11.17			
	16.11.17			
	17.11.17			
	18.11.17		Conf. Off. Football Team played 15th Div Sig. Transport & won 6 goals to 1.	
	19.11.17			
	20.11.17			
	21.11.17			
	22.11.17			
	23.11.17			
	24.11.17		Day off.	
	25.11.17		Football Team played 131 Fld Ambulance & lost 1 - 0.	
	26.11.17			
	27.11.17			

Army Form C. 2118.

WAR DIARY
or
INTELLIGENCE SUMMARY.
(Erase heading not required.)

Instructions regarding War Diaries and Intelligence Summaries are contained in F. S. Regs., Part II. and the Staff Manual respectively. Title pages will be prepared in manuscript.

124 Field Coy 18t

III

Place	Date	Hour	Summary of Events and Information	Remarks and references to Appendices
H.15.d.1.0.	28-11-17	10 am	As for 24th	
	29-11-17			
	30-11-17		1 Attacked Infantry wounded.	

C. S. Bray
Major
O.C. 124 Field Coy 18t

Secret

WO 25

Original War Diary
December 1917.

124th Field Coy R.E.
38th (Welsh) Division

124TH FIELD COMPANY, R.E.
No. ....
Date ....

Army Form C. 2118.

WAR DIARY
or
INTELLIGENCE SUMMARY. 124th Feed Coy RE.
(Erase heading not required.) December 1917

Place	Date 1917	Hour	Summary of Events and Information	Remarks and references to Appendices
Sheet 36 NW3				
H.15.d.1.0.	1.12.17	10am	Henri train Sector. Worked as November.	
	2.12.17		do	
	3.12.17		do Capt A.K Santer to RE School Rouchinchon on Course.	
	4.12.17		do No.1 Section Attached C.R.E. for Jack Area Work.	
	5.12.17		do	
	6.12.17			
	7.12.17			
	8.12.17			
	9.12.17			
	10.12.17		Company Relieved by Coy of Engineers of 2nd C.E.F. Proceeded to Armentières. Billets in Jute Factory. Took over work of Right Sub-sector Armentières Section, consisting of 2
	11.12.17		Shame to M.M.6. repairing trenches and reviving insular line.	
	12.12.17			
	13.12.17			

Army Form C. 2118.

WAR DIARY
or
INTELLIGENCE SUMMARY. 124th Fd. Cy. R.E.

(Erase heading not required.)

Instructions regarding War Diaries and Intelligence Summaries are contained in F.S. Regs., Part II. and the Staff Manual respectively. Title pages will be prepared in manuscript.

Place	Date	Hour	Summary of Events and Information	Remarks and references to Appendices
	14.12.17			
	15.12.17			
	16.12.17		Company move with to Bluejackets Armentiéres.	
	17.12.17			
	18.12.17			
	19.12.17		Company handed over work to 151 Fd.Cy.R.E. & returned to Steenbecq relieving Engineers of 2nd Cd.P. Billets at G.17.a.9.3. Work consists of concrete M.G.Bs.	
	20.12.17		No.1 Section rejoined Coy from CRE and replaced by No.4 Section	C.M.B
	21.12.17			
	22.12.17			
	23.12.17			
	24.12.17			
	25.12.17			
	26.12.17			

//

WAR DIARY
or
INTELLIGENCE SUMMARY

124 Field Coy. R.E.

Army Form C. 2118.
711

Place	Date	Hour	Summary of Events and Information	Remarks and references to Appendices
G.19.a.9.3.	27.12.17			
	28.12.17			
	29.12.17		Company went to Billets at H.19.d.1.1. with 11th Army to 4th Army area	
H.19.d.1.30.	30.12.17		Capt. A.M. Rankin repairs from Army	
	31.12.17			

C Bragd
Major R.E.
O.C. 124 Field Coy. R.E.

<u>Secret</u>

<u>Original War Diary.</u>

<u>124 Field Company R.E.</u>

<u>38th Division.</u>

Vol 26

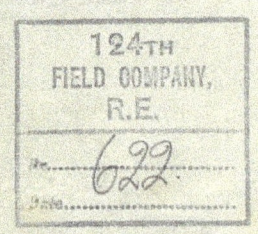

<u>January 1918.</u>

Army Form C. 2118.

WAR DIARY
or
INTELLIGENCE SUMMARY.

(Erase heading not required.)

124th Field Coy. R.E.

Instructions regarding War Diaries and Intelligence Summaries are contained in F.S. Regs., Part II. and the Staff Manual respectively. Title pages will be prepared in manuscript.

Place	Date	Hour	Summary of Events and Information	Remarks and references to Appendices
	January 1918			
Mag.d.11	1-1-18		"Leur Bois" Sector. Work on concrete M.G's. M.G.S. Capt. A.B. Soutar awarded M.C. 1-1-18. Sergt E. Warnock and Sapper	
	2-1-18			
	3-1-18			
	4-1-18			
	5-1-18			
	6-1-18			
	7-1-18			
	8-1-18			
	9-1-18			
	10-1-18			
	11-1-18			
	12-1-18		Company relieved by 89th Fd. Coy. R.E. 12 Bn. and move to	
L.29.b.2.b.			Neuf Berquin. Work on Corps Defences. No.1. Section	
Neuf Berquin			billets Croix du Bac. No.4 section Erquinghem. No. 3 section	
			Bac. St. Maur. No.2 section Transport at Neuf Berquin.	

Army Form C. 2118.

WAR DIARY
or
INTELLIGENCE SUMMARY.

(Erase heading not required.)

12th Field Coy. R.E.

Instructions regarding War Diaries and Intelligence Summaries are contained in F. S. Regs., Part II. and the Staff Manual respectively. Title pages will be prepared in manuscript.

Place	Date	Hour	Summary of Events and Information	Remarks and references to Appendices
Sheet 36NE	January 1918			
L.21.b.26	13		Company H.Q. moves to Sailly-sur-la-Lys at G.22.b.12.9.	
	14			
	15		Cont. on (Coy.) Defences. Sup. line.	
	16		Carrying of strong posts and connecting trenches in same between L.32.b. (Sheet 36 NE) and	
	17		B.24.c. (Sheet 36 NW.2) Dimensions of trenches are 4ft deep, 3ft wide	
	18		in bottom with slope of 1 in 1. Double Apron fence.	
	19		(18ft. seven.)	
	20			
	21			
	22			
	23			
	24			
	25			
	26			
	27			
	28			

Army Form C. 2118.

WAR DIARY
or
INTELLIGENCE SUMMARY.
(Erase heading not required.)

III

1st Field Coy. R.E.
12th Field Coy. R.E.

Instructions regarding War Diaries and Intelligence Summaries are contained in F. S. Regs., Part II. and the Staff Manual respectively. Title pages will be prepared in manuscript.

Place	Date	Hour	Summary of Events and Information	Remarks and references to Appendices
	29-1-15		As for 28th.	
	30-1-15			
	31-1-15			

C.G.Brough
Major R.E.
O.C. 12th Field Coy. R.E.

Army Form C. 2118.

WAR DIARY
or
~~INTELLIGENCE~~ SUMMARY.
(Erase heading not required.)

Instructions regarding War Diaries and Intelligence Summaries are contained in F. S. Regs., Part II. and the Staff Manual respectively. Title pages will be prepared in manuscript.

Place: 124th Field Coy. R.E.

Place	Date	Hour	Summary of Events and Information	Remarks and references to Appendices
Byblia Q	February 1918			
	1.		Reserve Division. Company employed on Corps Defences as per scheme for January 1918. Digging of Strong Pts practically caught up in hand. Connecting between posts commences.	
	2.		" Digging capacity of various units noted.	
	3.		" not above 10-15 C.ft. in Clay Loam taking however 3½-5½ hours.	
	4.		" Battalions have raised AisKicks and Country	
	5.		" equipment lost. Wiring: Screw of 1 NCO & 9 O.R., +	
	6.		" 1 NCO & 9 O.R. carrying, do 250 yds of double apron	
	7.		" fence with 6ft + 3ft wooden pickets completed in	
	8.		" 4 hours (any work). The importance of arranging	
	9.		" drainage and actually digging drains before	
	10.		" revetment of trenches was commenced, was	
	11.		" very noticeable.	
	12.			
	13.		10 work. Preparing handing over reports.	

Army Form C. 2118.

WAR DIARY
or
INTELLIGENCE SUMMARY

(Erase heading not required.)

122nd Field Coy. R.E.

Place	Date	Hour	Summary of Events and Information	Remarks and references to Appendices
G.H.Q.T.Q.	February 1918			
	14		Reserve Division. Relieved by 421st Field Coy. R.E. (37th Division). Company went to Armentieres & arrived from H.21 to H.Coy. R.E. Dauphine Lots. Armentieres Section. Coy. H.Q. at C.25.C.4.4. (Sheet 36 NW). Work consists of repairing Comp Sting concrete pillboxes, repairing demolition scheme to bridge area.	
	15		Coy. No.1. Section attacked 114 Engine for roads, and Etiquette in Dauphines.	
	16	"	"	
	17	"	"	
	18	"	1 Officer and 1 O.R. Killed, 1 O.R. died of wounds. Bombardy 17th.	
	19	"	Bombard 18th.	
	20	"	"	
	21	"	"	
	22	"	"	
	23	"	"	
	24	"	"	

Army Form C. 2118.

WAR DIARY
or
INTELLIGENCE SUMMARY.
(Erase heading not required.)

12+ fd. Coy. R.E.

Place	Date	Hour	Summary of Events and Information	Remarks and references to Appendices
Sheet 36NW	February 1918.			
C.25.C.A.4	25.	6" "		
	26.	Note. 24th		
	27.	" 9 "		
	28.	" " "		

E. O'Brazil
Major R.E.
O.C. 12x+ fd. Coy. R.E.

SECRET.

Original War Diary. March 1918.

121st Field Company Royal Engineers
38th (Welsh) Division

WAR DIARY
or
INTELLIGENCE SUMMARY.

127th Field Coy. R.E.

Vol 28

Army Form C. 2118.

(Erase heading not required.)

Place	Date	Hour	Summary of Events and Information	Remarks and references to Appendices
C25C44	March 1918			
	1		Bombino Actions. Armentieres Sector. Company working on C.T.'s drainage, concrete pillboxes, tackling bridges, arc lamps and preparing tank for demolition. No.1. Section attached 114th Infy. Brigade for work.	
	2		do	
	3		do	
	4		do	
	5		do	
	6		"	
	7		"	
	8		" 8 O.R. to hospital - wounded Gassed. (Shell)	
	9		"	
	10		"	
	11		"	
	12			

Army Form C. 2118.

WAR DIARY
or
INTELLIGENCE SUMMARY. 12th Field Coy R.E.

(Erase heading not required.)

Instructions regarding War Diaries and Intelligence
Summaries are contained in F.S. Regs., Part II.
and the Staff Manual respectively. Title pages
will be prepared in manuscript.

Place	Date	Hour	Summary of Events and Information	Remarks and references to Appendices
	March 1918			
	13.		Work as to 12th, 6 O.R. to hospital wounds (shell)	
	14.		" " 5 " " "	
	15.		" " " " "	
	16.		" " " " "	
	17.		10pm + 5 " " " "	
	18.		18. " Major Brazel prociderance to U.K. 16/3/18	
			Gas Casualties were caused by	
			gas shells falling on the entrance of No1. dston	
			dug-out, during a gas shell bombardment by the	
			enemy.	
	19.		Work as for 18th –	
	20.		"	
	21.		"	
	22.		"	
	23.		"	
	24.		"	

Army Form C. 2118.

WAR DIARY
or
INTELLIGENCE SUMMARY.
(Erase heading not required.)

Place	Date	Hour	Summary of Events and Information	Remarks and references to Appendices
	25		Took ao to 24th	
	26		"	
	27		"	
	28		Company preparing for relief.	
	29		"	
	30		Capt. H.H. Soutar proceeds to join 98th Field Coy. R.E. for duty as O.C.	
	31		Company move from Brumetra, relieved by 207. H. Coy. R.E. 31st Division to Steenbecque for entrainment. Dismounted personnel to Ionio transport by road. Lieut. 20 Jones joins Coy for duty.	

H. Mather
Lieut R.E.
a/O.C. 132 th Coy R.E.

38th Div.
V.Corps.

WAR DIARY

124th FIELD COMPANY, R.E.

A P R I L

1 9 1 8

Army Form C. 2118

1st Kent Coy R.E.

Vol 29

WAR DIARY
or
~~INTELLIGENCE SUMMARY.~~
(Erase heading not required.)

Place	Date	Hour	Summary of Events and Information	Remarks and references to appendices
BOESINGHEM	April 1918			
	1.		Whole Company entrains at Steenecque 5.0 p.m.	
	2.		joins 113th Brigade Group and detrains at Boulleux. Major C.H. Bruges rejoins Coy. from leave.	
	3.		Company proceeded by march route to La Nicogne.	
	4.		Doing Infantry and Engineer Training.	
	5.		— do. — under orders to move at 1 hours notice.	
La Nicogne	5.		Company proceed to HERISSART vid. 114th Bdy. Brigade Group, but on arrival billetting accommodation not available and return to La Nicogne.	
	6.		Company doing Infantry and Engineer Training	
	7.		— do —	
	8.		— do —	
	9.		— do —	
	10.		— do —	
	11.		— do —	
	12.		Left La Nicogne at 1 a.m. and proceeded to the Line	

WAR DIARY

Army Form C. 2118

1st Fd. Coy. R.E.

Place	Date	Hour	Summary of Events and Information	Remarks and references to Appendices
	June 1918			
	12.		Arriving at V.9.b. 7.3. (Senlis) at 4 p.m. Lines at U. 30. to 5.8. Warloy.	
	13.		Company move camp to V.8. 6. 2.8. Work in the line consist of trench digging, wiring (double apron fence) on Old Green Line from W. 13. 6. 8.8. to V. 2n. d. 7.9. and Corps Line from V. 18. 6. 6.9. 6 V. 18. C. 1.0. (V Corps., 3rd Army.) Work being done at night.	
	14.		Work aa to 13 t.	
	15.		Company move to lines at Contay.	
	16.		Work aa to 13th.	
	17.		— do. —	
	18.		— do. —	
	19.		— do. — One Sapper wounded.	
	20.		— do. — " (Cpl) wounded.	
	21.		— do. — one " "	

Army Form C. 2118.

WAR DIARY
or
INTELLIGENCE SUMMARY. 123rd Field Coy. R.E.
(Erase heading not required.)

Instructions regarding War Diaries and Intelligence Summaries are contained in F. S. Regs., Part II. and the Staff Manual respectively. Title pages will be prepared in manuscript.

Place	Date	Hour	Summary of Events and Information	Remarks and references to Appendices
V.6.c.2.4.	April 1918			
	22.		2nd Lt. 2nd Lt. R.G.S. Carolin R.E. attd. from 151 Coy. R.E.	
	23.		"	
	24.		"	
	25.		" Lt. G.D. Jones to be A/Capt. from 23/4/18 whilst 2nd in command of Company.	
	26.		"	
	27.		" Commenced mine dugouts M.14 & M.44 and M.15 a 36.	
	28.		" One attacked Infantry Aid of wounds.	
	29.		"	
	30.		"	

C.H.Bragg.
Major R.E.
O.C. 123rd Field Coy. R.E.

SECRET.

124TH FIELD COMPANY, R.E.

Original War Diary.
May 1918.

124th Field Company Royal Engineers
38th (Welsh) Division

Army Form C. 2118.

WAR DIARY
or
INTELLIGENCE SUMMARY
(Erase heading not required.)

12nd Field Tech. Coy. R.E.

Place	Date	Hour	Summary of Events and Information	Remarks and references to Appendices
V.6.b.2.8.	1.5.16	-	Work continued on Old Trench Line digging New C.T. + continue wiring. 2 sections attached "B" Brigade to work on Deep Dug-outs at W.13.a.2.6. to Left & Right Batt. H.Q.	Divisional W/5c/16 /113c Sw'57/ASE
	2.5.16		"	
	3.5.16		"	
	4.5.16		"	
	5.5.16		"	
	6.5.16		"	
	7.5.16		"	
	8.5.16		"	
	9.5.16		Attached Infy. N.C.O. wounded.	
	10.5.16		2 Sappers wounded	
	11.5.16		"	
	12.5.16		"	
	13.5.16		"	

Army Form C. 2118.

WAR DIARY
or
INTELLIGENCE SUMMARY.
(Erase heading not required.)

Bn. 1st Coy. R.E.

Instructions regarding War Diaries and Intelligence Summaries are contained in F.S. Regs., Part II. and the Staff Manual respectively. Title pages will be prepared in manuscript.

Place	Date	Hour	Summary of Events and Information	Remarks and references to Appendices
V.B.2.S.	14.5.18		Oct for 13th	
	15.5.18		"	
	16.5.18		" 1 Officer + 1 N.C.O. of American Engineers attached for instruction	
	17.5.18		"	
	18.5.18		" One R.E. killed 2 Sappers, 2 Attached Infantry wounded.	
	19.5.18		"	
	20.5.18		" Company relieved & took over the line by 205th Coy. 7/0.1/6.16.4ft.	
			and commence work on senior Defences under C.E. V Corps Sw.5.p.S.E.	
			digging new trenches + wiring. Americans rejoin their unit.	
			As for 20th.	
	21.5.18		"	
	22.5.18		"	
	23.5.18		"	
	24.5.18		" Attached Infantry rejoin their units.	
	25.5.18		"	
	26.5.18		"	
	27.5.18		"	

Army Form C. 2118.

WAR DIARY
or
INTELLIGENCE SUMMARY. 124 Fd. Coy. R.E.
(Erase heading not required.)

Place	Date	Hour	Summary of Events and Information	Remarks and references to Appendices
V.8.6.2.8.			Aston 29th	
	28.5.18		"	
	29.5.18		" Held meeting of N.C.Os & representatives (Sapper Bryant) to explain details of Scheme for Demobilisation & Reconstruction & to explain Educational Classes at the held on Active Service. Meeting to reassemble in 6 days to discuss particulars of Educational Classes & Suggested Subjects for same.	
	30.5.18			
	31.5.18			
	31.5.18			

C.W. Brazel.
Major R.E.
O.C. 124 Fd Coy R.E.

SECRET.

Original War Diary.
June 1916.

124th Field Company Royal Engineers
38th (Welsh) Division

Army Form C. 2118.

WAR DIARY or INTELLIGENCE SUMMARY.
(Erase heading not required.)

181 Kd. Coy. R.E.

Instructions regarding War Diaries and Intelligence Summaries are contained in F. S. Regs., Part II. and the Staff Manual respectively. Title pages will be prepared in manuscript.

Place	Date	Hour	Summary of Events and Information	Remarks and references to Appendices
	June 1915			
V.8.b.2.9.	1st		Company at work on Sentie defences and CE V Corps. trenches digging and wiring. Working parties of 1 Batt. Welsh Regt. and 'B' Coy 19th Welsh (Pioneers).	
Sh. 51c SE.	2.		do	
	3.		do	Major C.H. Brazil awarded Military Cross + 62390 Cpl Anthony Watkins "Kings birthday Honours."
	4.		do	
	5.		Preparing for relief by and handing over.	
	6.		Company relieved by 2nd + 7th Fd Coy R.E. (63rd Divn) and proceeds to P. 36. b. 9.2. (forward H.Q.) and relieves 2nd Fd Coy R.E.	
			Rems H.Q. Transport lines at O. 30. d. 3. 5. Work on trenches, wiring and mines, dug-outs. No. 2 Section in reserve	
	7.		do	
	8.		do	
	9.		do	
	10.		do	
	11.		forward H.Q. move to P. 35. b. 9. 4. No. 2 Section relieved by No. 1.	

T/134. Wt. W708—776. 500030. 4/15. Sir J. C. & S.

Army Form C. 2118.

WAR DIARY
or
INTELLIGENCE SUMMARY.
(Erase heading not required.)

 124 Feed S Coy. R.E.

Instructions regarding War Diaries and Intelligence Summaries are contained in F.S. Regs., Part II. and the Staff Manual respectively. Title pages will be prepared in manuscript.

Place	Date	Hour	Summary of Events and Information	Remarks and references to Appendices
P.35 c 9 d.	June 1918			
	12	Ack to 11.		
	13	do	Lieut. J. Forsyth granted leave to U.K. from 13.6.18 to 27.6.18.	
	14	do		
	15	do		
	16	do		
	17	do	No 1 Section relieved by No. 4 Section in reserve	
	18	do		
	19	do		
	20	do		
	21	do	8 Sappers accompanied 2nd Batt on a raid nr to Aveluy Wood as a demolition party, each carrying a mobile charge, only one Shelter C'not be found and the one blown in. No Casualties. 4.50. +72. Sapper J. Syphenton awarded a D.C. Certificate.	
	22	Ack to 20.	No. 4 Section relieved by No. 3 Section in reserve	
	23	do		
	24	do		

Army Form C. 2118.
711

WAR DIARY
or
INTELLIGENCE SUMMARY.
(Erase heading not required.)

12th Field Coy. R.E.

Place	Date	Hour	Summary of Events and Information	Remarks and references to Appendices
P.32.b.9.a.	25th		June 1915.	
	26th		As for 24th	
	27th		do.	
	28th		do. forward H.Q. move to P.26. Central	
P.26 Central	29th		do.	
	30th		do.	

C. W. Brazil
Major R.E.
O.C. 12 or 7th Coy. R.E.

SECRET.

Original War Diary
July 1918.

124th Field Company Royal Engineers
38th Division.

WAR DIARY
or
INTELLIGENCE SUMMARY.

Army Form C. 2118.

127th Field Coy R.E. I

9/1132

Place	Date	Hour	Summary of Events and Information	Remarks and references to Appendices
P26 Cent.	July 1918			
	1st		Work on trenches-wiring, &c. Lewis raid to September. Rear H.Q. Transport lines at 0.30.a.25.	
	2nd		do	
	3rd		do	
	4		do	
	5		do	
	6		"	
	7		"	
	8		"	
	9		"	
	10		"	
	11		1 NCO + 9 Sapper accompany 2nd R.W.F. on raid as a demolition party into the enemy trenches in France. Each carrying a 20lb Mobile charge. Several cellars dug-outs + Emplacements were demolished. 6x6.14. Sapper Gabst awarded M.M.	
	12		aston 163.	

Army Form C. 2118.

WAR DIARY
or
INTELLIGENCE SUMMARY.
(Erase heading not required.)

Instructions regarding War Diaries and Intelligence Summaries are contained in F.S. Regs., Part II. and the Staff Manual respectively. Title pages will be prepared in manuscript.

Mtd. Col. Coy R.E.

Place	Date	Hour	Summary of Events and Information	Remarks and references to Appendices
			July 1918	
Rfb. Cow.	13.	a.a. to rfb.		
	14.	do.		
	15.	do.		
	16.	do.		
	17.	do.	Preparing for relief.	
	18.	do.	do.	
	19.		Relieved by 118/4th Coy. + 124/7th Fd. Coy. of 17th & 63rd Divns.	
	20.		Company now to P.O.W. camp Lastencourt. T.6.a.22.	
	21.		Drill bridging demolitions etc.	
	22.		do.	
	23.		do. Major C.H. Brazel grants leave 6 p.m. 22.7.18 to 4.8.18.	
			do. on action attack on 2nd N.Z. Bde or 15.	
	24.		in M.M.C. Harponville.	
	25.		a.a. to rfb. do.	
	26.		do. Lieut. R.E. Sparks.	

Army Form C. 2118.

WAR DIARY
or
INTELLIGENCE SUMMARY.
(Erase heading not required.)

1st Fd. Coy. R.E.

Instructions regarding War Diaries and Intelligence Summaries are contained in F. S. Regs., Part II. and the Staff Manual respectively. Title pages will be prepared in manuscript.

Place	Date	Hour	Summary of Events and Information	Remarks and references to Appendices
T.b.d.2.2.	27		As for 26th. Training etc.	
	28		do.	
	29		do.	
	30		do.	
	31		do.	

BJJones Capt R.E.
for Major R.E.
O.C. 1st Field Coy. R.E.

Secret.

Original

War Diary.

12th Field Company R.E.

August 1918.

Army Form C. 2118.

WAR DIARY
or
~~INTELLIGENCE SUMMARY~~

(Erase heading not required.)

12th Spr. Coy. R.E.

Place	Date	Hour	Summary of Events and Information	Remarks and references to Appendices
Shr. 5/D	August 1918			
T.6.d.22	1st		Company with Division in reserve. Training. 2 Sections at work on Div. H.Q. Dug-ot 6 at U.11.a. (Harponville)	
	2nd		do	
	3rd		do	
	4th		do	
	5th		do	
	6th		Company relieves and is relieved by 17th Fd. Coy. R.E. Coy. H.Q. at P.36.a.19. Raincourt Lines U.11.C.2.7. Work on 'MOIR' Pillboxes, constructing 'lean' trencher + revetting. One two in same renovating existing trenches and repairing forward road. No. 3 Section attached to 113 Brigade for work.	
	7th		do	
	8th		do	
	9th		do	

Army Form C. 2118.

WAR DIARY
or
INTELLIGENCE SUMMARY.

(Erase heading not required.)

12th Field Coy R.E.

Instructions regarding War Diaries and Intelligence Summaries are contained in F.S. Regs., Part II. and the Staff Manual respectively. Title pages will be prepared in manuscript.

Place	Date	Hour	Summary of Events and Information	Remarks and references to Appendices
Sheet 27 S.E.			August 1918.	
P.36.a.1.9.	10th		At H.Q.	
	11th		do	
	12th		do	
	13th		do	
	14th		do	
	15th		Whole Company Concentrated on repairing of forward roads.	
	16th		do	
	17th		do	
	18th		do	
	19th		do	
	20th		Repairing of forward roads. One Section working on Pill box.	
	21st		do	
	22nd		No.1 Section (Lt. Vander) reported to 104th Batt. Welsh Regt. No.2 Section (Lt. Poole) reported to 13 R Batt En.F. No.3 Section (Lt. Malinson) reported to 14th Batt. En.F. and concerned with Infantry and assisted in consolidating USNA REDOUBT. No.4 Section (Lt. Pany) moved forward

Army Form C. 2118.

WAR DIARY
or
INTELLIGENCE SUMMARY.
(Erase heading not required.)

124 Field Coy RE

Place	Date	Hour	Summary of Events and Information	Remarks and references to Appendices
Sheet 57D SE			August 1918	III
P.36.a.1.9	22nd		With 1 Batt, 19th R.W.F.	
	23rd		No 1 Section Ad beach 13th 7th Batt. W. Welsh Regt.	
			No 2 Section Advanced with Infantry & avoided Consolidation.	
			1 Officer wounded, 1 O.R. Killed, 1 O.R. wounded.	
			No 3 Section Erected barricade on road near USNA REDOUBT. 1 O.R. wounded	
			No 4 Section Moved forward with 1 Batt.	
	24th		No 1 Section advanced with Infantry commenced consolidation, but moved forward before completion. 2 O.R. wounded	
			No 2 Section advanced with 16th Batt 18th J.F. and assisted in consolidation.	
			Section Sergt & 1 Sapper Killed, 1 Sapper wounded.	
			No 3 Section advanced with 1 Batt.	
			No 4 Section moved forward with 1 Batt.	
N.15.a.7.3	25th		Coy H.Q. moved to N.15.a.7.3.	
			No 1 Section advanced with Infantry.	
			No 2 Section reported Coy at 113 Bde H.Q.	
			No 3 Section do.	

WAR DIARY
or
INTELLIGENCE SUMMARY.

Army Form C. 2118.

(Erase heading not required.)

124 Field Coy. R.E.

Place	Date	Hour	Summary of Events and Information	Remarks and references to Appendices
Sh 57c S.E.			August 1918.	
V.15.a.7.3	25th		No 4 Section moved forward with Batt. and searched for wells.	
A.17 & 16.95	26th		Coy rear H.Q. moved to N.11.b. 16.95.	
			No 1 Section advanced with Infantry.	
			No 4 Section moved forward with Batt.	
X.10.d.5.5	27th		Coy rear H.Q. moved to X.10.d.5.5.	
			No 1 Section advanced with Infantry. 1st/8th Warden wounded. 1 Sapper killed.	
			No 4 Section moved forward with Batt. but unable to consolidate, section kept.	
			Returned.	
X.13.d.2.7	28th		Coy rear H.Q. moved to X.13.d.2.7. Sheet 57c. S.W.	
			No 1 Section repair Coy.	
			No 4 Section C.O.	
			Coy forward H.Q.	
	29th		Dug portion of defensive line from High Wood to Longueval S.11 & S.10.d. Sheet 57c. S.W.	
	30th		Commenced work on road from Bazentin le Petit to Longueval.	
X.10.d.5.5			Coy rear H.Q. moved to X.10.d.5.5	

Army Form C. 2118.

WAR DIARY
or
INTELLIGENCE SUMMARY

(Erase heading not required.)

124 Field Coy RE

Place	Date	Hour	Summary of Events and Information	Remarks and references to Appendices
Fr 57D SW X10d 8.6	August 1918			V
	31st		Work on roads from Bazentin le Petit to Longueval	

W Toye Capt RE
OC 124 Field Coy RE

Army Form C. 2118.

WAR DIARY
or
INTELLIGENCE SUMMARY

1st Field Coy. R.E.

(Erase heading not required.)

Place	Date	Hour	Summary of Events and Information	Remarks and references to Appendices
S.W. of D. X.10.d.5.5.	September 1918			
	1st		Company employed on roads from Bazentin le Petit to Longueval	
	2nd		do. Transport move to T.16.a.1.5 8.14.b.3.6. Company move to T.16.a.1.5 works on road Ginchy to Lesboeufs.	
	3rd		do. Making reconnaissance & for wells and looking for booty.	
	4th		ditto	
	5th		do. Company and Transport move to 5.4.a.4.6. on Division being relieved by 21st Division.	
	6th		Coy. at rest.	
	7th		do.	
	8th		do. 1 Section removing enemy booty Trap from Inf. Bgd.	
	9th		Coy. move to Sub. Reception at N.15.b.1.6. work on same, repairing and renewing the camp.	
	10th		do.	
	11th		Coy. moved to work on roads toward Sub. v. Brigade H.Q. and near 6. P.32.d.2.3. Transport lines in W.I.D. Relieves Coy. of N.Z. Division.	

Army Form C. 2118.

WAR DIARY
or
INTELLIGENCE SUMMARY.
(Erase heading not required.) 1st Field Coy. R.E.

Instructions regarding War Diaries and Intelligence Summaries are contained in F.S. Regs., Part II. and the Staff Manual respectively. Title pages will be prepared in manuscript.

Place	Date	Hour	Summary of Events and Information	Remarks and references to Appendices
	September 1915			
A.22.d.2.3.	12		Work on roads and forward water points. Brigade & Divl. H.Q.	
	13.		ditto.	
	14.		ditto.	
	15.		ditto.	
	16.		Company proceed to work on Batts. H.Q. in Q.33.b. & Q.34.a. remaining there the night. 2 Sections 1st For.Coy R.E. under O.C. arrive for work on Brigade H.Q.	
			do. Company return to H.Q. on completion of work.	
	17.		Standing to.	
	18.		Work on forward roads.	
	19.		do. No.1. working on C.R.E's Hear H.Q.	
	20.		do. do.	
	21.		Return.	
	22.		Company working on roads.	
	23.		Resting.	
	24.		Commenced work on Batts. H.Qrs. P.S.6.	

Army Form C. 2118.

WAR DIARY
or
INTELLIGENCE SUMMARY. 1st Field Coy. R.E.
(Erase heading not required.)

Vol 34

Instructions regarding War Diaries and Intelligence Summaries are contained in F. S. Regs., Part II. and the Staff Manual respectively. Title pages will be prepared in manuscript.

Place	Date	Hour	Summary of Events and Information	Remarks and references to Appendices
B.32.d.2.3	September 1918			
	25		Work on Battn. H.Q. in P.25.b.	
	26		do. work compl 6 6.	
	27		Training e.t.	
	28		" Company move to N.20.a.98 Rawton Lines N.13.a.51	
	29 & 30		do. for reserve	
			do — " Gas proofing dugouts.	

D Irvey Capt R.E.
f.o.C. 1st Fd. Coy. R.E.

WAR DIARY or INTELLIGENCE SUMMARY.

1st Fd. Coy. RE

Place	Date	Hour	Summary of Events and Information	Remarks and references to Appendices
W.v.a.9	October 1st		Company each Division in reserve, employed on Divl. H.Q. and proofing dugouts etc. Major C.H. Bruger acting Liaison officer with right Divn. to bridging Escaut Canal.	
	2.		— do —	
	3.		— do —	
	4.		Company move to F.8.a.3.1.	
	5.		Company move to S.25.b.1.5. Standing to. Bridging Canal. Transport lines move to F.8.a.3.1. as for 3rd.	
	6.		— do —	
	7.		— do — Transport lines move to X.2+C.1.3. Company move to Villers Outreaux. Bridging completed. Nos 1, 2+3 R. Sections attached to Montgomery and advance with Infantry in attack on Villers Outreaux Malincourt on morning of 8th. H. Sappers harassed.	

Army Form C. 2118.

WAR DIARY
or
INTELLIGENCE SUMMARY.
(Erase heading not required.)

12th Field Cy R.E.

Place	Date	Hour	Summary of Events and Information	Remarks and references to Appendices
T.14.9.0.	October			
	9.		2 & 3 Sections rejoin company. Work on road repairs, filling in craters etc. Transport lines moved to T.5.c (Malincourt)	
	10.		— do —	
	11.		Company transport moves to Berty. In reserve with Division.	
	12.		Company proceed to Troisvilles but return to Berty same day. Employed on roads etc.	
	13.		— do —	
	14.		No. 1 Section proceed to Troisvilles to work on heavy bridging on River Selle.	
	15.		Remainder of Coy. move to Troisvilles. Bridging & Mine marauders an sappeurs maines.	
	16.		— do —	
	17.		— do —	
	18.		do	
	19.		do & Transporting bridging parts from dump to site of erection.	

WAR DIARY or INTELLIGENCE SUMMARY

Army Form C. 2118.

10th Field Coy R.E.

Place	Date	Hour	Summary of Events and Information	Remarks and references to Appendices
T.35.c.2.8	October 20		Coy to 19 C.	
	21.		O.C. to for bridge erected on line Selle in face of heavy Artillery & M.G. fire. Not successfully accomplished.	
	22.		Company at rest.	
	23.		Doing repairs to Rev. Bde. H.Q. 1 O.R. Answered M.M.	
	24.		Company move to Montay K.22.d.15.15 and work on R.H.Q. Naufort — Troisvilles T.35.c.2.8.	
	25.		Work on A.H.D.	
	26.		"B" Echelon transport men to Montay K.22.d.15.15. "C" Croix T.21.c.5.4. No.1 section attd to 123 Fd. Coy. No.3. to 151 Fd Coy. R.E.	
	27.		Coy to 76 C. Coy working on dugouts	
	28.	"	do	1 O.R. Answered M.M.
	29.	"	do	1 Sapper wounded.
	30.	"	do	

Army Form C. 2118.

WAR DIARY
or
INTELLIGENCE SUMMARY.
(Erase heading not required.)

12th Field Coy R.E.

Place	Date	Hour	Summary of Events and Information	Remarks and references to Appendices
S25 c.2.6	October 31st		Nos 2 & 4 Sections working on dugouts Tillinyan Crater. Nos 1 & 3 Section repair Coy.	

D. Jones Capt RE
2/o O.C. 12th Field Coy RE.

SECRET.

Original War Diary.
November 1918.

124th Field Company Royal Engineers
38th (Welch) Division

124TH FIELD COMPANY, R.E.

Army Form C. 2118.

WAR DIARY
or
INTELLIGENCE SUMMARY.
(Erase heading not required.)

12th Field Coy R.E.

Vol 36

Place	Date	Hour	Summary of Events and Information	Remarks and references to Appendices
Sht 57d NE Q.19.C.5.4. R.25.d.10.10	November 1916			
	1st		Company working on road cratero. 108 killed 9 Died of wounds 108 wounded	
	2nd		As for 1st	
	3rd		As for 1st	
Sht 57d NW A.1.C.3.5	4th		Company moved to A.1.C.3.5. Company working on road cratero at Eaucourt. Positions of Teams and Drivers placed at disposal of 3rd Division.	
	5th		As for 4th "B" Echelon move to 7.91.6.5.4.	
	6th		As for 5th "B" Echelon move to A1.6.3.5	
C.8.C.9.7.	7th		Coy (with "B" Echelon) move to C.8.C.9.7. Company working on Eridge approach.	
Sht 57d S.W. U.29.b.25.85	8th		"A" "B" Echelon Amalgamated move for the Oise.	
	9th		Coy move to U.29.b.25.85. Company employed on Bridges.	
Sht 57d S.E. X.26.6.2.5	10th		Coy working on Bridge approach.	
			Coy move to X.26.b.2.5. Work on road Crati Bridge.	
	11th		Hostilities cease 11 a.m.	
	12th		- do - Lieut R.P. Findlay awarded M.C.	
	13th		- do -	
	14th		- do -	

T2134. Wt. W708—776. 500000. 4/15. Sir J. C. & S.

Army Form C. 2118.

WAR DIARY
or
INTELLIGENCE SUMMARY. 1st Field Coy. R.E.

(Erase heading not required.)

Instructions regarding War Diaries and Intelligence Summaries are contained in F. S. Regs., Part II. and the Staff Manual respectively. Title pages will be prepared in manuscript.

Place	Date	Hour	Summary of Events and Information	Remarks and references to Appendices
	November 1917			
SH 51 SE X26.b.2.S.	15th			
	16th		Company moved to Choises X.14.b.6.0. and are employed on same work.	
	17th		- do -	
	18th		- do -	
	19th		- do -	
	20th		- do -	Work on Crabs & Bigets completed.
	21st		Preparing for move.	
	22nd		Coy. move to Beliamont U.21.c.5.4. Training and Insure overhauling of Coy. equipment.	
	23rd		- do -	
	24th		- do -	
	25th		- do - Coy parade for inspection by O.C.	
	26th		Training etc. Coy. (with 123 Coy, 151 Coy Pioneers) reviewed by G.O.C. 38th Welsh Division. 62431. Sgt. Cowgave 236857. Spr. P. Telford 108017 Awarded Good Conduct Certificates.	

Army Form C. 2118.

171

1st Field Coy R.E.

WAR DIARY
or
INTELLIGENCE SUMMARY.
(Erase heading not required.)

Instructions regarding War Diaries and Intelligence Summaries are contained in F. S. Regs., Part II. and the Staff Manual respectively. Title pages will be prepared in manuscript.

Place	Date	Hour	Summary of Events and Information	Remarks and references to Appendices
U.21.C.5.4.	November 1918			
	27th		Training C.E.	
	28th		do	
	29th		do	
	30.		Transport preparing for move to Amiens area.	

C.W. Brazil
Major R.E.
O.C. 1st Fd. Coy. R.E.

SECRET.

Original War Diary.
December 1918.

124th Field Company R.E.
38th (Welsh) Division

Army Form C. 2118.

WAR DIARY
or
INTELLIGENCE SUMMARY. 156 th Field Coy. R.E.

(Erase heading not required.)

Place	Date	Hour	Summary of Events and Information	Remarks and references to Appendices
U.21.C.5.4	1.		Company in Perlimount. Training etc. Transport here for Amiens area.	
	2.		Company (dismounted) move to Southampton.	
	3.		Company entrains at Salouches for Amiens area.	
	4.		Detrains at Fuxeu for tramway and billets for the night.	
	5.		Company and Transport arrives in Park Novelles.	
	6.		Move to Querrieu and relieved 276 Fd Coy R.E.	
Querrieu	7.		Work commences on R.A. camps and Head quarters.	
	8.		As for 8. Work on Camps, erecting Nissan Huts, stables etc.	
	9.		do	
	10.		do	
	11.		do	
	12.		do	
	13.		do 20 O.R. sent to England for Coal mining.	
	14.		- do -	

Army Form C. 2118.

WAR DIARY
or
INTELLIGENCE SUMMARY. 1st Fd. Coy. R.E.

(Erase heading not required.)

Instructions regarding War Diaries and Intelligence Summaries are contained in F. S. Regs., Part II. and the Staff Manual respectively. Title pages will be prepared in manuscript.

Place	Date	Hour	Summary of Events and Information	Remarks and references to Appendices
Querrieu	December 1916			
	15		Work on R.A. Camp.	
	16		do –	
	17		do –	
	18		do –	
	19		do –	
	20		Major C.H. Brazel granted leave to U.K.	
	21		do –	
	22		do –	
	23		do –	
	24		do –	
	25		Xmas day holiday.	
	26		Work on Camp.	
	27		do –	
	28		do	
	29		(Red) hunting	
	30		Work on Camp	
	31		do	

J Tours
Capt R.E.
a/O.C. 1st Fd. Coy. R.E.

Secret

Original War Diary.
January 1919

124TH FIELD COMPANY R.E.

124 Fd Coy Royal Engineers
38th (Welsh) Division

Army Form C. 2118.

WAR DIARY
or
INTELLIGENCE SUMMARY.
(Erase heading not required.)

Instructions regarding War Diaries and Intelligence Summaries are contained in F. S. Regs., Part II. and the Staff Manual respectively. Title pages will be prepared in manuscript.

1st Fd. Coy. R.E.

Place	Date	Hour	Summary of Events and Information	Remarks and references to Appendices
Quiévrain	1		Work erecting & fitting out R.A. Camp	
	2			
	3			
	4			
	5			
	6			
	7		} ditto	
	8			
	9			
	10			
	11			
	12			
	13			
	14			
	15			
	16			

Army Form C. 2118.

238~~
1/4 Fd. Coy R.E.

WAR DIARY
or
INTELLIGENCE SUMMARY.
(Erase heading not required.)

182 38

Place	Date	Hour	Summary of Events and Information	Remarks and references to Appendices
Quarries	17		January 1916	
	18		Work on R.A. Camp.	
	19			
	20			
	21			
	22			
	23		ditto	
	24			
	25			
	26		New Years Honours & Awards:	
	27		Capt. D.O. Jones - Mentioned in Despatches	
	28		62756 C.S.M. J. Grant "M.S.M."	
	29		H28/15 Sergt. J. Browning "D.C.M."	
	30			
	31			

D O Jones
Capt. R.E.
O/C 1/4 Fd. Coy R.E.

Original War Diary.
February 1919

124th Field Company. Royal Engineers
38th (Welsh) Division

Army Form C. 2118.

WAR DIARY
or
INTELLIGENCE SUMMARY. 1st Feed Coy. R.E.

(Erase heading not required.)

Instructions regarding War Diaries and Intelligence Summaries are contained in F. S. Regs., Part II. and the Staff Manual respectively. Title pages will be prepared in manuscript.

Place	Date	Hour	Summary of Events and Information	Remarks and references to Appendices
			February 1919.	
Auvin	1st		Company working on Headquarters and R.A. Camp.	
	2		"	
	3		"	
	4		"	
	5		"	
	6		"	
	7		"	
	8		H.R.H. the Prince of Wales visits the Company.	
	9			
	10			
	11			
	12		Coy. move to billets at Quevy. Company employed on various jobs and at the workshops.	
	13			
	14			
	15		"	
	16			

Army Form C. 2118.

WAR DIARY
or
INTELLIGENCE SUMMARY. 12th Field Coy. R.E.

(Erase heading not required.)

Instructions regarding War Diaries and Intelligence Summaries are contained in F.S. Regs., Part II. and the Staff Manual respectively. Title pages will be prepared in manuscript.

Place	Date	Hour	Summary of Events and Information	Remarks and references to Appendices
Busny	17		February 1919.	
	18		no form tr.	
	19		"	
	20		"	
	21		Lieut. Warwick Jones ret'd for duty ander 21.2.19.	
	22		"	
	23		"	
	24		Capt. D.O. Jones Lt. R.P. Quialay leave to Paris 24.2.19 to 28.2.19.	
	25		"	
	26		"	
	27		Company absent Cadre "B" Strength	
	28		"	

J. Richardson M/Lt.E
12th Field Coy. R.E.

Secret. Original
War Diary.

124th Field Coy, R.E.

March 1919.

Army Form C. 2118.

WAR DIARY
INTELLIGENCE SUMMARY
(Erase heading not required.)

194 Field Company R.E.

Place	Date	Hour	Summary of Events and Information	Remarks and references to Appendices
Bussy Les Thomer	March 1919			
	1st		Work on electric lighting plant, Pont Noyelle. Erecting cover over R.A.S.C. Dump Allonville. Also hutting.	
	2nd		Do	
	3rd		Do	
	4th		Constructing 2" pipe line at Pont Noyelle. Also hutting. Lewis at R.F.A. Camp.	
	5th		As for 4th. Lt. E.G. Findlay, MC, transferred to 11th Railway Construction Coy.	
	6th		As for 4th.	
	7th		2/Lt. Makinson transferred to G.B.D. On 6th & 7th Coy transport, with exception of Officer Mess car and 1 lorry, parked at Cadre Camp G.21.S.4.	
	8th		As for 4th.	
	9th		Maintaining Guard on transport at G.21.S.4.	
	10th		Re-erecting Mess Hut at Cadre Park G.21.S.4. Repairs of and improvements to Camp at Blangy-Tronville.	
	11th		As for 9th.	

Army Form C. 2118.

WAR DIARY
or
INTELLIGENCE SUMMARY
(Erase heading not required.)

194 Field Coy R.E.

Place	Date	Hour	Summary of Events and Information	Remarks and references to Appendices
Bouzey-les-Graoum			March 1919.	
	12th		C/o for gib	
	13th		do	
	14th		do	
	15th		do	
	16th		do	
	17th		do	
	18th		do	
	19th		do	
	20th		Company returned to Camp A.	
	21st		Completion of making space for maintaining	
	22nd		space at Camp Camp.	
	23rd		C/o for 91st	
	24th		— do —	
	25th		— do —	
	26th		— do —	
	27th		— do —	

WAR DIARY
or
INTELLIGENCE SUMMARY.
(Erase heading not required.)

Army Form C. 2118.
III

187th R. Field Coy R.E.

Place	Date	Hour	Summary of Events and Information	Remarks and references to Appendices
	March 1919.			
Bray-s- 28th			As for 27th	
Somme 29th			do	
30th			do	
31st			do	

W. Richardson
2/Lt R.E.
a/O.C 187th Field Coy R.E.

Secret

Original

War Diary

124th Field Coy R.E.

April 1919

124TH
FIELD COMPANY,
R.E.
No. 1954

Vol 41

WAR DIARY
INTELLIGENCE SUMMARY.
(Erase heading not required.)

Army Form C. 2118

194th Field Coy R.E.

Place	Date	Hour	Summary of Events and Information	Remarks and references to Appendices
Ongay & Dacourt		April 1919		
	1		Overhauling & checking Company Equipment, maintaining Guard at Cara Camp etc.	
	2		do for 101	
	3		— do —	
	4		— do —	
	5		— do —	
	6		— do —	
	7		— do —	
	8		— do —	
Vecquemont	9		do for 101. Company move to Vecquemont	
	10		— do —	
	11		— do —	
	12		— do —	
	13		— do —	
	14		— do —	
	15		— do —	

WAR DIARY
or
INTELLIGENCE SUMMARY.

(Erase heading not required.)

Army Form C. 2118.

194th Field Coy R.E.

Place	Date	Hour	Summary of Events and Information	Remarks and references to Appendices
Vacquinant	16		April 1919.	
	17		Coys. 1st. Repairing Camp at Colony	
	18		do - do -	
	19		do - do -	
	20		do - do -	
	21		do - do -	
	22		do - do -	
	23		do - do -	
	24		do - do -	
	25		do - do -	
	26		do - do -	
	27		do - do -	
	28		do - do -	
	29		do - do -	
	30		do - do -	

D. Tong Capt.
O.C. 194 Field Coy R.E.

WAR DIARY
or
INTELLIGENCE SUMMARY.
(Erase heading not required.)

124th Field Coy. R.E.

From 1st May to 1st June 1919.

Army Form C. 2118.

Place	Date	Hour	Summary of Events and Information	Remarks and references to Appendices
Vicarnmoor	1 May 1919		Mounting guard at Coan Camp	
	2		As for 1st	
	3		Do	
	4		Do	
	5		Do	
	6		Do	
	7		Do	
	8		Do	
	9		Do	
	10		Do	
	11		Do	
	12		Do	
	13		Do	
	14		Do	
	15		Do	
	16		Do	

WAR DIARY
or
INTELLIGENCE SUMMARY.

Army Form C. 2118.

17th Field Coy R.E.

Place	Date	Hour	Summary of Events and Information	Remarks and references to Appendices
Vicquemont	17	May 1919	As for 1st	
	18		Do	
	19		Do also supervising dismantling of a heavy bridge at Meaulte	
	20		Do	
	21		Do Repairs Road Bray to Guerrieu	
	22		Do Do	
	23		Do Do	
	24		Do Do	
	25		As for 1st also Repairs Road Bray to Guerrieu	
	26		Do Do	
	27		Do Do	
	28		Do Do	
	29		Do Do	
	30		Do Do	
	31		Do Do	

JJones Capt
OC 17th Field Coy R.E.

Army Form C. 2118.

WAR DIARY
or
INTELLIGENCE SUMMARY.
(Erase heading not required.)

1/2t Field Company R.E.

Instructions regarding War Diaries and Intelligence Summaries are contained in F. S. Regs., Part II. and the Staff Manual respectively. Title pages will be prepared in manuscript.

Place	Date	Hour	Summary of Events and Information	Remarks and references to Appendices
Abbeville	1	June 1919	Mr Continuing Guard at Cable Cargo. Also repairing road from to Grenier.	
	2		Do	
	3		Do	
	4		Repairing road.	
	5		Repairing road.	
	6		Available men proceed with for disposal.	
	7		Remainder of Company (returnables) proceed to 6t (Midland) Division Rhine Army. Capt. D. Jones conducting party to Rhine afterwards to proceed U.K. for disposal. Dispersal of Unit Complete.	

D Jones Capt RE
O.C. 192 Field Coy RE

T2134. Wt. W708—776. 500,000. 4/15.

www.ingramcontent.com/pod-product-compliance
Lightning Source LLC
Chambersburg PA
CBHW081526160426
43191CB00011B/1689